curry ingredients
1 cinnamon sticks
2 onions
3 fresh mint
4 fresh chillies
5 fresh lemon grass
6 fresh root ginger
7 dried rampé leaves
8 garlic
9 ornamental chillies
10 dried curry leaves
11 peppercorns
12 lentils
13 dried daun salam leaves
14 dried lemon grass
15 fresh coriander

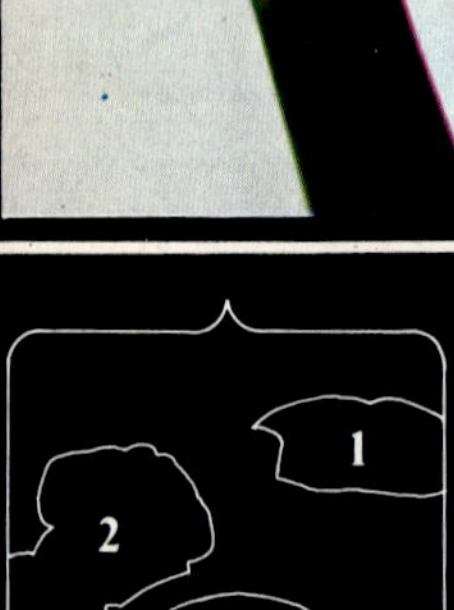

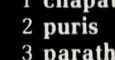

1 chapatis
2 puris
3 parathas

far eastern cookbook

EDITOR
 ELIZABETH SEWELL

PHOTOGRAPHER
 REG MORRISON

DESIGNER
 BRUNO GRASSWILL

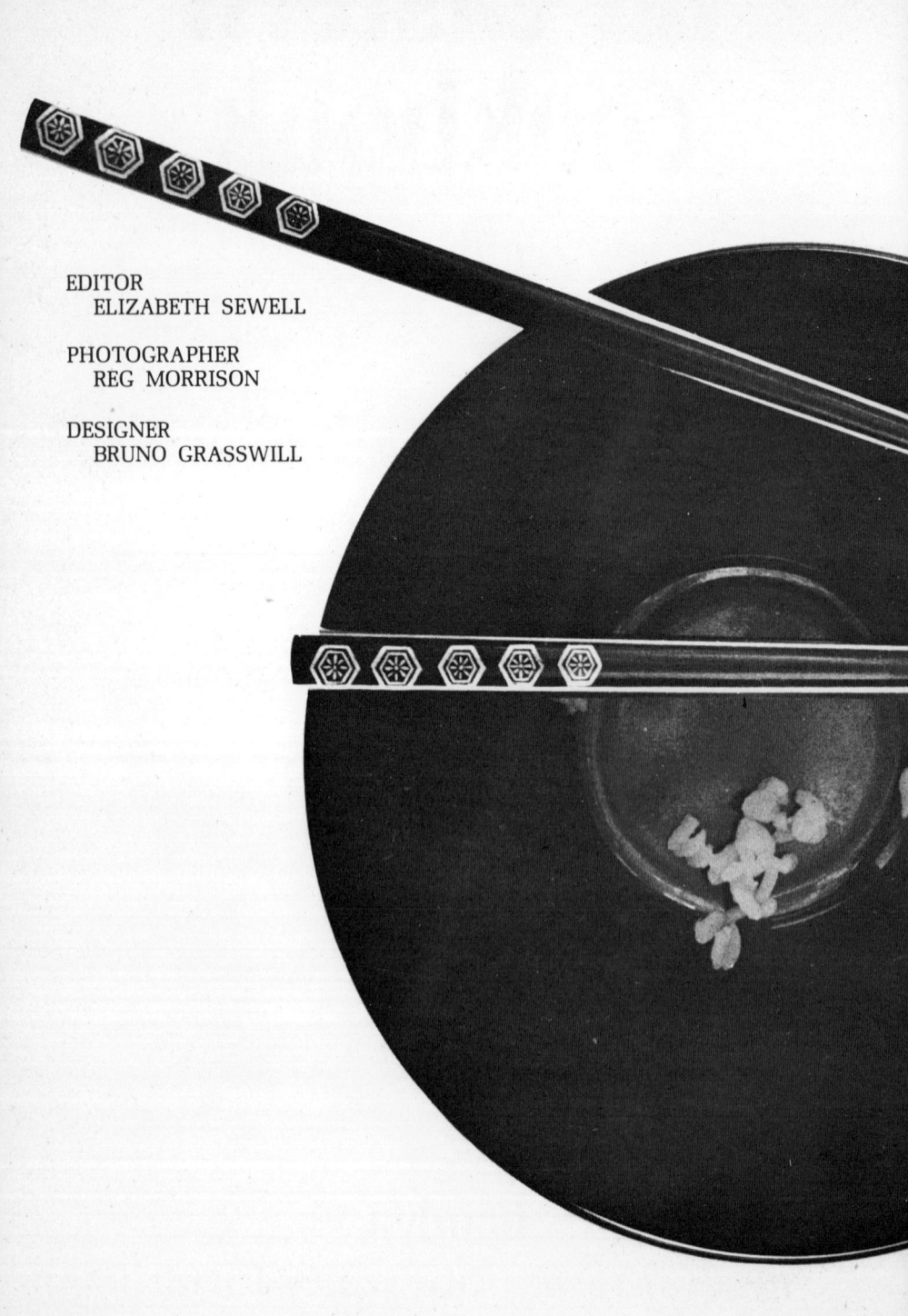

far eastern cookbook

charmaine solomon

hamlyn
london·newyork·sydney·toronto

The editor would like to thank the following for their help and co-operation in the preparation of and photography for this book:

David Jones' Ltd.
Saytin Fong and Co.
Thomas South Pacific (Australia) Pty. Ltd.

First published by Paul Hamlyn Pty. Ltd. 1972
©Copyright Paul Hamlyn Pty. Ltd. 1972
This edition published by the Hamlyn Publishing Group Limited 1973
London • New York • Sydney • Toronto
Hamlyn House, Feltham, Middlesex, England
ISBN 0 600 38095 5
Printed in Korea

contents

india 10

ceylon 31

burma 50

thailand 60

indonesia 65

malaysia and singapore 76

china and japan 89

entertaining 101

menus 112

accompaniments 114

glossary 115

index 119

guide to weights and measures

The weights and measures (non-Metric) used throughout this book refer to those adopted by The Standards Association of Australia. All spoon and cup measures are level unless otherwise stated.

Housewives in AMERICA, CANADA and BRITAIN using this book will find the following table a helpful guide to teaspoon, tablespoon and cup measures.

Please note that the Australian, American and British teaspoons all have a 5-millilitre capacity; the Australian standard tablespoon (20 millilitres) is larger than the American Standard tablespoon (15 millilitres) and the British Standard tablespoon (17.7 millilitres).

It is also important to know that one American pint is equal to 16 fluid ounces whereas the pint used in Australia and Britain is 20 fluid ounces. The standard measuring cup used in this book has a capacity of 8 fluid ounces, which is equal to ⅖ of the Imperial pint.

Australian	American	British
1 teaspoon	1 teaspoon	1 teaspoon
1 tablespoon	1⅓ tablespoons	1 tablespoon
2 tablespoons	3 tablespoons	2 tablespoons
3 tablespoons	4 tablespoons	3½ tablespoons
4 tablespoons	4⅔ tablespoons	4½ tablespoons
5 tablespoons	7 tablespoons	5½ tablespoons
6 tablespoons	8½ tablespoons	7 tablespoons
scant ¼ cup	scant ¼ cup	3 tablespoons
⅓ cup	⅓ cup	4 tablespoons
½ cup	½ cup	6 tablespoons (scant ¼ cup)
⅔ cup	⅔ cup	¼ PINT (8 tablespoons)
1 cup	1 cup	scant ½ pint
1¼ cups	1¼ cups	½ pint
2 cups (generous ¾ pint)	2 cups (1 pint)	generous ¾ pint
2½ cups (1 pint)	2½ cups	1 pint (20 fluid ounces)

metric guide

Because there is no exact conversion between metric and imperial units, we suggest the housewife replaces 1 ounce with 25 grams and 1 fluid ounce with 25 millilitres.

In order to preserve the correct ratio of ingredients in a recipe, strict conversion should not be applied. Each imperial measure—whether a pound, pint or cup, should be related to the base unit of the imperial system—the ounce or fluid ounce. The number of ounces and fluid ounces should be multiplied by 25 to give the metric quantities, thereby preserving the proportions.

This has been done in the table provided.

Ounces and Fluid Ounces	Grams and Millilitres	Ounces and Fluid Ounces	Grams and Millilitres
1	25	7	175
2	50	8 (cup)	200
3	75	10	250
4	100	12	300
5	125	16 (1 pound) (1 US pint)	400
6	150	20 (1 Imperial pint)	500

Liquid proportions should be adjusted if necessary to maintain correct consistencies.

Abbreviations:

Kilogram: kg
Gram: g
Millilitre: ml
Centimetre: cm

pronunciation

Saying Eastern names is very easy as they are completely phonetic. This guide to vowel sounds will help:
a as in ah
e as in met
i as in pin
ie as in pie
o as in vote
u as oo in moot

oven temperature guide

This is an approximate guide only. Different makes of cookers vary and even the same make of cooker can give slightly different individual results at the same temperature. If in doubt with your particular cooker, do refer to your own manufacturer's temperature chart. It is impossible in a general book to be exact for every cooker but the following is a good average guide in every case.

The following chart also gives approximate conversions from degrees Fahrenheit to degrees Celsius (formerly known as Centigrade). This chart can be used for conversion of recipes which give oven temperatures in metric measures.

Description of oven	Fahrenheit	Celsius	Gas Mark
Very cool	225	110	¼
	250	130	½
Cool	275	140	1
	300	150	2
Moderate	325	170	3
	350	180	4
Moderately hot	375	190	5
	400	200	6
Hot	425	220	7
	450	230	8
Very hot	475	240	9

cooking equipment

If you are serious about cooking curries and don't possess an electric blender, think seriously about getting one. My blender is in constant use.

It grinds curry ingredients and spices to a fine powder. It crushes peppercorns; grinds coconut; blends onions, garlic, herbs and other ingredients to a smooth purée and makes curry paste. In fact, it does all the jobs that are done on grinding stones, with a mortar and pestle, or in grinding mills in Eastern homes. If you like to cook Asian food in a country where household help is limited, then you need (believe me, you do need) an electric blender with a good, powerful motor.

There are a few other moderately priced gadgets I depend on very much. One is a very sharp Chinese chopper. This chopper has a large, thin blade that slices and chops ingredients with great ease. It slices onions paper thin and is also useful for slicing and shredding meat, fish, poultry and vegetables necessary for some Eastern dishes. Choppers can be bought in small and large sizes and most of them have dark metal blades. They don't look very beautiful, but they do get the job done.

A good, sharp, stainless steel grater is another thing I use all the time. I use it to grate carrot, garlic and ginger.

metric guide

Because there is no exact conversion between metric and imperial units, we suggest the housewife replaces 1 ounce with 25 grams and 1 fluid ounce with 25 millilitres.

In order to preserve the correct ratio of ingredients in a recipe, strict conversion should not be applied. Each imperial measure—whether a pound, pint or cup, should be related to the base unit of the imperial system—the ounce or fluid ounce. The number of ounces and fluid ounces should be multiplied by 25 to give the metric quantities, thereby preserving the proportions.

This has been done in the table provided.

Ounces and Fluid Ounces	Grams and Millilitres	Ounces and Fluid Ounces	Grams and Millilitres
1	25	7	175
2	50	8 (cup)	200
3	75	10	250
4	100	12	300
5	125	16 (1 pound) (1 US pint)	400
6	150	20 (1 Imperial pint)	500

Liquid proportions should be adjusted if necessary to maintain correct consistencies.

Abbreviations:

Kilogram: kg
Gram: g
Millilitre: ml
Centimetre: cm

pronunciation

Saying Eastern names is very easy as they are completely phonetic. This guide to vowel sounds will help:
a as in ah
e as in met
i as in pin
ie as in pie
o as in vote
u as oo in moot

oven temperature guide

This is an approximate guide only. Different makes of cookers vary and even the same make of cooker can give slightly different individual results at the same temperature. If in doubt with your particular cooker, do refer to your own manufacturer's temperature chart. It is impossible in a general book to be exact for every cooker but the following is a good average guide in every case.

The following chart also gives approximate conversions from degrees Fahrenheit to degrees Celsius (formerly known as Centigrade). This chart can be used for conversion of recipes which give oven temperatures in metric measures.

Description of oven	Fahrenheit	Celsius	Gas Mark
Very cool	225	110	¼
	250	130	½
Cool	275	140	1
	300	150	2
Moderate	325	170	3
	350	180	4
Moderately hot	375	190	5
	400	200	6
Hot	425	220	7
	450	230	8
Very hot	475	240	9

cooking equipment

If you are serious about cooking curries and don't possess an electric blender, think seriously about getting one. My blender is in constant use.

It grinds curry ingredients and spices to a fine powder. It crushes peppercorns; grinds coconut; blends onions, garlic, herbs and other ingredients to a smooth purée and makes curry paste. In fact, it does all the jobs that are done on grinding stones, with a mortar and pestle, or in grinding mills in Eastern homes. If you like to cook Asian food in a country where household help is limited, then you need (believe me, you do need) an electric blender with a good, powerful motor.

There are a few other moderately priced gadgets I depend on very much. One is a very sharp Chinese chopper. This chopper has a large, thin blade that slices and chops ingredients with great ease. It slices onions paper thin and is also useful for slicing and shredding meat, fish, poultry and vegetables necessary for some Eastern dishes. Choppers can be bought in small and large sizes and most of them have dark metal blades. They don't look very beautiful, but they do get the job done.

A good, sharp, stainless steel grater is another thing I use all the time. I use it to grate carrot, garlic and ginger.

lamb kebabs on pilau
onion sambal

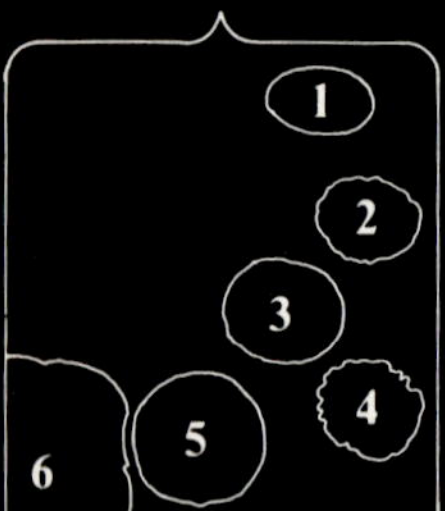

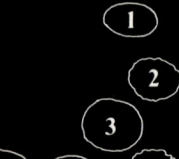

1 dhal
2 brinjal bartha
3 cucumber salad
4 podina chatni
5 bean curry
6 chapatis

preface

For years I've been giving recipes to friends. I'm always pleased when they tell me the results are marvellous, the recipes surprisingly easy. 'Why don't you put them in a book,' they say. Well, at last, it seems I have done so. It makes me happy to know that through my book many more people will be able to explore the delights of Eastern food.

The recipes are authentic, but the methods are those I have perfected in my kitchen in Australia without the benefit of those wonderfully willing servants we are blessed with in the East, who chop and grind and prepare ingredients for the mistress who decides to do a little cooking.

I am grateful to many people who gave me an interest in cooking—
...first there was my Aunt Muriel—a gentle person whose artistry in making cakes, confectionery and other delights is one of my childhood memories. She was an accomplished pianist too and from her I learned that good cooking is an art as creative as painting or music.

...my father's sisters, Miss Elva and Miss Claribel Poulier, with whom I lived for many years, are renowned in Ceylon for their prize-winning chutneys, pickles and everyday cooking of an extremely high standard. From them I learned meticulous attention to detail.

...my mother and grandmother, born and brought up in Burma, and both superb cooks. My grandmother also lived for many years in India and shared with me her knowledge of Indian food. By their good cooking at home they taught me to have high standards in my own kitchen.

...Margaret Fulton, Cookery Editor of *Woman's Day*, has encouraged and helped me since we met eight years ago. She said, 'You'll just have to find time to do this book, Charmaine, no matter what else you don't do.' From her I learned that you put everything else aside when you have an important project on hand. (Margaret, there's dust under the beds and a room full of ironing!)

...my children—gourmets each and every one. Even the baby prefers his steak marinated Japanese-style. From them I have learned, too late, not to show off to your kids—they then have to be fed in the style to which they've become accustomed.

Last, but most important of all, I am grateful to my husband, Reuben. A musician by profession, he is a truly creative cook himself. If it had not been for his wide knowledge of Eastern food and appreciation of my efforts, I would not have been encouraged to make a special study of the subject. His enthusiasm and help have made this book possible. From him I learned that George Meredith, who said, 'Kissing don't last, cookery do,' was not altogether right. Kissing **do** last—as long as the cookery is up to scratch!

I hope you enjoy cooking and eating this food as much as I've enjoyed writing the recipes for you.

Charmaine Solomon

india

I have always loved Indian food, but only learned to cook it when my grandmother came to stay with us. She had lived for many years in India and when she prepared a meal I enjoyed it right from the moment I stepped in the door and smelt the appetising fragrance, to the time I had to stop eating because there simply was no room for more.

My husband is a keen cook too, and the three of us had some great times in the kitchen. Nana was a born homemaker, a born mother—one of those women who glory in being a woman. She taught me many things—among them to cook Indian food so that I have been paid the supreme compliment of being told it is 'even better than Mogul Street'. (Mogul Street is famous for its kebabs, parathas and other Indian specialities).

India is a land of contrasts and this is also true of its food. It varies from the rich, mild dishes of North India to the hot, spiced preparations of the South.

Average Westerners, asked what food they associate with India, will name curry. But every spiced dish is not a curry, and curry is not just one dish. It embraces a whole range of dishes, each distinctly different according to the spices and herbs used in varying combinations. This clever use of spices is the outstanding feature of Indian cookery. Subtle or pungent, hot or mild, there is something to suit every palate.

Rice is the staple food in some provinces of India, while in others the daily bread is the chapati, made from whole wheat flour. These round, flat discs are cooked on a hot griddle for a few minutes only.

In India, religions impose many food taboos. Muslims will not eat pork. Hindus will not eat beef. Buddhists will not take life and so will not even crack an egg. Many are vegetarians. Whatever their rules in regard to diet, most Indians obey them implicitly.

Indian vegetarian cooking is in a class by itself. It includes superb curries; barthas (purees) and bhajis (fried vegetables); bhajias (fritters) and vadais (crisp rissoles of lentils and peas); home-made bread with spiced vegetable fillings; rich sweetmeats made with vegetables and fruits, others made with lentil flour and still others based on milk and clarified butter. All are flavoured with spices and are rich with almonds and pistachio nuts.

Many Indians eat with their fingers, even at formal meals, using the right hand only. Done expertly, it is neat and graceful. When eating Indian breads, there is no other way. Tear off a piece of chapati or paratha, use it to scoop up the accompaniment, fold over neatly and place in the mouth. No trick to it.

When eating rice and curry, however, many do prefer to use a dessertspoon and fork. Rice is served first in the centre of the plate. Then various curries and accompaniments are placed around it. The rice is the base against which curries may be savoured, and only one curry should be tasted with each mouthful of rice.

The recipes that follow merely scratch the surface of India's richly varied cuisine. But if you cook and enjoy these dishes, they will have opened the door to a whole new world of flavour.

chapatis

Flat discs of unleavened wholemeal bread, with a delightful flavour and chewy texture.

Yield: 20-24

Ingredients	Metric	Imperial
Fine wholemeal or roti flour	600 ml	3 cups
Salt	1-1½ teaspoons or to taste	1-1½ teaspoons or to taste
Ghee or oil (optional)	1 tablespoon	1 tablespoon
Lukewarm water	200 ml	1 cup

Place wholemeal flour in a mixing bowl, reserve approximately 100 ml (½ cup) for rolling the Chapatis. Mix salt through the flour in the bowl, then rub in ghee or add oil, if used. Add water all at once and mix to a fairly soft dough. Knead dough for at least 10 minutes. (The more it is kneaded, the lighter the bread will be.) Form dough into a ball, cover with clear plastic and stand for 1 hour or longer. (Dough wrapped in clear plastic and left overnight makes very light and tender Chapatis.)

Shape dough into balls about the size of a large walnut. Roll out each one on a lightly floured board (using reserved wholemeal flour) to a circular shape, as thin as a French crêpe. After rolling out Chapatis, heat a griddle plate or heavy based frying pan until very hot. Place chapati on griddle and leave for about 1 minute. Turn and cook other side a further minute. Press lightly around the edges of the chapati with a folded tea towel or with an egg slice. This encourages bubbles to form and makes the Chapatis light. As they are cooked, wrap in a clean tea towel until all are ready. Serve immediately with butter, dry curries or vegetable dishes.

puris

(pronounced poo-rees)
Deep Fried Wholemeal Bread

Proceed as for Chapatis (see above). When all the dough is rolled out, heat approximately 2.5 cm (1-inch) of oil in a deep frying pan. When a faint haze rises from the oil, fry Puris, one at a time, over a moderate heat. Spoon hot oil continually over the cooking puri until it puffs and swells. Turn over and fry other side in the same way. When both sides are pale golden brown, drain on absorbent paper.

Serve immediately with curries and bhajis.

parathas

Flaky Wholemeal Bread

Probably the favourite variety of Indian bread, Parathas are rich, flaky and deliciously flavoured with ghee. Kebabs and Parathas is a combination which is quite famous. A dear old friend of my grandmother taught me her method of rolling and folding the Parathas—the easiest and most successful one I've tried.

Yield: 12-14

Ingredients	Metric	Imperial
Fine wholemeal flour	300 ml	1½ cups
Plain white flour	300 ml	1½ cups
Salt	1½ teaspoons	1½ teaspoons
Water	200 ml	1 cup
Ghee	6-8 tablespoons	6-8 tablespoons
Extra ghee	for cooking	for cooking

Sieve wholemeal flour, white flour and salt into a mixing bowl and rub in 1 tablespoon of the ghee. Add water, mix and knead dough as for Chapatis (see page 11). Cover dough with clear plastic and stand aside for 1 hour.

Divide dough into 12-14 equal portions and roll each into a smooth ball. Melt ghee over a low heat and allow to cool. Roll each ball of dough on a lightly floured board into a very thin circular shape. Pour 2 teaspoons of the melted ghee in the centre of each and spread lightly with the hand. With a knife, make a cut from the centre of each circle to the outer edge. Starting at the cut edge, roll the dough closely into a cone shape. Pick it up, press the apex of the cone and the base towards each other and flatten slightly. You will now have a small, roughly circular lump of dough again. Lightly flour the board again and roll out the dough very gently, taking care not to press too hard and let the air out at the edges. The Parathas should be as round as possible, but not as thinly rolled as the first time.

Cook on a hot griddle liberally greased with extra ghee, turning Parathas and spreading with more ghee, until they are golden brown. Serve hot with grilled kebabs, Onion Sambal (see page 25) and Podina Chatni (see page 24).

Note: 600 ml (3cups) roti flour may be used instead of the wholemeal and plain flour.

pilau

Rice cooked in stock with spices.
Serves: 4-5

Ingredients	Metric	Imperial
Chicken	400 g	1 lb
Cardamom pods	4	4
Peppercorns	10	10
Salt	4½ teaspoons	4½ teaspoons
Bay leaves	2	2
Onion	1	1
Cloves	3	3
Basmati rice	500 ml	2½ cups
Ghee	5 tablespoons	5 tablespoons
Extra onion, finely sliced	1 large	1 large
Powdered saffron or saffron strands	good pinch ¼ teaspoon	good pinch ¼ teaspoon
Garlic, crushed	2 cloves	2 cloves
Finely grated fresh root ginger	½ teaspoon	½ teaspoon
Garam masala	½ teaspoon	½ teaspoon
Ground cardamom	½ teaspoon	½ teaspoon
Rose water	3 tablespoons	3 tablespoons
Sultanas	50 ml	¼ cup

Make a strong, well-flavoured chicken stock by simmering chicken in water to cover with cardamom pods, peppercorns, 2 teaspoons salt, bay leaves and the onion stuck with cloves. Simmer for approximately 2 hours. Cool slightly, strain stock and measure 800 ml (4 cups). Remove chicken meat from bones, cut into bite-size pieces and set aside. (If time does not permit the making of home-made stock, combine 800 ml (4 cups) of boiling water and 4 large chicken stock cubes, mix together thoroughly).

Wash rice thoroughly in water, drain in a colander and allow to dry for at least 1 hour. Heat ghee in a large saucepan and fry sliced onion until golden. Add saffron, garlic and ginger and fry for 1 minute, stirring continuously. Add rice and fry 5 minutes longer over a moderate heat, stirring with a slotted metal spoon. (This prevents breaking the long delicate grains of rice which add so much to the appearance of this dish.) Add hot stock, garam masala, cardamom, remaining salt, rose water, sultanas and reserved chicken pieces, stir well. Cover pan with a tightly fitting lid and cook over a very low heat for 20 minutes. Do not uncover saucepan or stir rice during cooking time.

When rice is cooked, remove from heat and stand, uncovered, for 5 minutes. Fluff up rice gently with a fork and place in a serving dish, again using a slotted metal spoon. Garnish with 50 ml (¼ cup) fried almonds, 200 ml (1 cup) hot cooked peas and 4 hard-boiled eggs cut in halves.

mogul biriani

Biriani is a very rich pilau, usually layered with a spicy mutton or chicken savoury mixture and steamed very gently so that the flavours blend while the rice and meat remain in separate layers.

It is the masterpiece of many Eastern cooks and the central dish at festive dinners. Here is a recipe for a lamb biriani, suitable for serving at a party.

Serves: 12-15
Cooking time: 20-30 minutes
Oven temperature: 160-170°C (325-350°F)

Ingredients	Metric	Imperial
Lamb Savoury:		
Boned leg of lamb	1.6-2 kg	4-5 lb
Ghee	5 tablespoons	5 tablespoons
Onions, sliced	3 large	3 large
Garlic, chopped	6 cloves	6 cloves
Finely chopped fresh root ginger	1½ tablespoons	1½ tablespoons
Curry powder	6 tablespoons	6 tablespoons
Salt	4 teaspoons	4 teaspoons
Lemon juice	2 tablespoons	2 tablespoons
Garam masala	1 teaspoon	1 teaspoon
Ground cardamom	1 teaspoon	1 teaspoon
Fresh chillies	2	2
Chopped mint	100 ml	½ cup
Tomatoes, peeled and chopped	400 g	1 lb
Chopped fresh coriander	2 tablespoons	2 tablespoons
Pilau (see page 13)		
Extra ghee	1 tablespoon	1 tablespoon

Lamb Savoury: Trim all excess fat from lamb and cut lean lamb into large cubes. Heat ghee in a saucepan and fry the onion, garlic and ginger until soft and golden. Add curry powder and fry 1 minute longer, then add salt and lemon juice. Add cubed lamb and fry, stirring continuously, until it is thoroughly coated with the spice mixture. Add garam masala, cardamom, whole chillies, mint and tomato.

Cover and cook over a very low heat for approximately 1 hour, stirring occasionally. When lamb is tender and gravy very thick and almost dry, turn off heat and remove whole chillies. Sprinkle with chopped coriander.

Pilau: (See page 13). Double all quantities and leave cooking times the same. Make a strong stock substituting 2-3 lamb shanks for chicken. Measure 1.6 litres (8 cups) stock.

When Pilau is cooked, allow to cool slightly. Melt extra ghee in a large ovenproof casserole and put in one-third of the Pilau, packing it in lightly. Spread half the lamb savoury over, taking it right to the edges of the casserole. Cover with half the remaining Pilau. Repeat layers. Put lid on casserole and place in a moderately slow oven for 20-30 minutes.

To serve, garnish as for Pilau.
For special occasions, add blanched pistachio nuts and edible silver leaf to the garnish in traditional Indian style.

kitchri

Savoury Rice and Lentils

Serves: 4

Ingredients	Metric	Imperial
Rice	200 ml	1 cup
Red lentils	200 ml	1 cup
Ghee or butter	2½ tablespoons	2½ tablespoons
Onions, finely sliced	2 large	2 large
Hot water	1 litre	5 cups
Salt	2½ teaspoons	2½ teaspoons
Garam masala	1½ teaspoons	1½ teaspoons

Wash rice and drain well. Wash lentils well, removing any that float to the surface, then drain thoroughly.

Heat ghee in a saucepan and fry onion gently until golden brown. Remove half the fried onion and reserve. Add rice and lentils to pan and fry, stirring continuously, for approximately 3 minutes. Add hot water, salt and garam masala. Bring to the boil, cover and simmer over a very low heat for 20-25 minutes or until rice and lentils are cooked. Do not lift the lid or stir during cooking time.

Serve hot, garnished with the reserved fried onion.

kofta curry

Meatball Curry

This is one of the tastiest curries. Seasonings are mixed in the meat balls which are then cooked in a spicy gravy.

Serves: 6

Ingredients	Metric	Imperial
Koftas:		
Finely minced meat, beef or lamb	400 g	1 lb
Onion, finely chopped	1 medium	1 medium
Garlic, crushed	1 clove	1 clove
Finely grated fresh root ginger	¼ teaspoon	¼ teaspoon
Fresh green or red chilli, seeded and finely chopped	1	1
Chopped fresh coriander or mint	2 tablespoons	2 tablespoons
Salt	1½ teaspoons	1½ teaspoons
Garam masala	1 teaspoon	1 teaspoon
Egg, well-beaten	1	1
Oil	for frying	for frying
Gravy:		
Ghee or oil	2 tablespoons	2 tablespoons
Onions, finely chopped	2 medium	2 medium
Garlic, finely chopped	2 cloves	2 cloves
Finely chopped fresh root ginger	1 tablespoon	1 tablespoon
Ground turmeric	1 teaspoon	1 teaspoon
Garam masala	1 teaspoon	1 teaspoon
Chilli powder (optional)	1 teaspoon	1 teaspoon
Tomatoes, chopped	2	2
Salt	1 teaspoon	1 teaspoon
Lemon juice	1 teaspoon	1 teaspoon
Chopped fresh coriander or mint	1 tablespoon	1 tablespoon

Koftas: Mix minced meat, onion, garlic, ginger, chilli, coriander, salt and garam masala together. Shape into balls the size of small walnuts. Dip in beaten egg and deep fry in hot oil until golden brown. Drain on absorbent paper.

Gravy: In a large heavy saucepan, heat ghee and fry onion, garlic and ginger until soft and golden. Add turmeric, garam masala and chilli powder if used and stir for 1 minute. Add tomato, salt, lemon juice and stir well. Add koftas. Cover and simmer for 20-25 minutes or until gravy is thick. Add chopped coriander for last 5 minutes of cooking time. Serve with boiled rice, vegetable curries and other accompaniments.

egg curry

Make gravy as for Kofta Curry (see page 16). Simmer until thick and fairly smooth, approximately 20 minutes.

Add 6 hard-boiled eggs, cut in halves lengthways. Simmer until heated through, spooning gravy over them. Serve with boiled rice, pickles and pappadams.

fish curry

Make gravy as for Kofta Curry (see page 16), adding 1 tablespoon desiccated coconut. Simmer for approximately 20 minutes.

Add 800 g (2 lb) fresh jewfish or cod fillets, cover and simmer over a low heat for 10-12 minutes or until fish is cooked. Serve immediately with boiled rice or Kitchri (see page 15).

Note: If a blender is available, mix desiccated coconut with 100 ml (½ cup) water and blend at top speed for 30 seconds before adding to gravy.

tali machchi

Indian Style Fried Fish

Serves: 4-5

Ingredients	Metric	Imperial
Firm white fish fillets	400 g	1 lb
Plain flour	3 tablespoons	3 tablespoons
Pea flour	3 tablespoons	3 tablespoons
Salt	1½ teaspoons	1½ teaspoons
Garam masala	1 teaspoon	1 teaspoon
Ground turmeric	½ teaspoon	½ teaspoon
Oil	for frying	for frying
Egg, well beaten	1	1

Wash and dry fish fillets. Mix flour, pea flour, salt, garam masala and turmeric together. Heat oil in a deep frying pan until smoking hot. Dip fish fillets into beaten egg, then lightly coat with the flour mixture. Fry quickly until golden brown on both sides. Drain on absorbent paper and serve immediately with boiled rice, pickles and Brinjal Bartha (see page 21).

lamb kebabs

Serves: 6-8

Ingredients	Metric	Imperial
Boned leg of lamb	1.6 kg	4 lb
Garlic	1 large clove	1 large clove
Salt	2 teaspoons	2 teaspoons
Finely grated fresh root ginger	1½ teaspoons	1½ teaspoons
Freshly ground black pepper	1 teaspoon	1 teaspoon
Ground turmeric	1 teaspoon	1 teaspoon
Ground coriander	1 teaspoon	1 teaspoon
Ground cummin	1 teaspoon	1 teaspoon
Crushed dried curry leaves	1 teaspoon	1 teaspoon
Crushed dried oregano leaves	1 teaspoon	1 teaspoon
Soy sauce	1 tablespoon	1 tablespoon
Sesame oil	1 tablespoon	1 tablespoon
Peanut oil	2 tablespoons	2 tablespoons
Lemon juice	1 tablespoon	1 tablespoon

Trim excess fat from lamb and cut meat into 2.5 cm (1-inch) cubes, place in a large bowl. Crush garlic with salt and combine with remaining ingredients, mix thoroughly. Pour over lamb and stir, making sure each piece of meat is covered with the spice mixture. Cover bowl and refrigerate for at least 3 hours, or as long as 4 days.

Thread 4-5 pieces of meat on each skewer and cook under a hot grill, allowing approximately 5 minutes on each side. When nicely browned, serve hot with boiled rice or Parathas (see page 12), accompanied by Onion Sambal (see page 25) and Podina Chatni (see page 24).

lamb curry

Serves: 6-8

Ingredients	Metric	Imperial
Boned shoulder of lamb	1.2 kg	3 lb
Ghee or oil	2 tablespoons	2 tablespoons
Onions, chopped	3 large	3 large
Garlic, chopped	3 cloves	3 cloves
Finely chopped fresh root ginger	1 tablespoon	1 tablespoon
Curry powder	2 tablespoons	2 tablespoons
Salt	3 teaspoons	3 teaspoons
Vinegar or lemon juice	2 tablespoons	2 tablespoons
Tomatoes, chopped	3 large	3 large
Fresh red or green chillies	2	2
Chopped fresh mint	2 tablespoons	2 tablespoons
Garam masala	1 teaspoon	1 teaspoon
Chopped fresh coriander or extra mint	1 tablespoon	1 tablespoon

Cut lamb into squares. Heat ghee in a saucepan and gently fry onion, garlic and ginger until soft and golden. Add curry powder, salt, vinegar, stir thoroughly. Add lamb and cook, stirring continuously, until lamb is coated with the spice mixture. Add tomato, chillies and mint, cover and cook over a very low heat for 1¼ hours or until lamb is tender, stirring occasionally. The tomatoes should provide enough liquid for the meat to cook in, but if necessary, add a little hot water, approximately 100 ml (½ cup), just enough to prevent meat from sticking to saucepan. Add garam masala and chopped coriander for last 5 minutes of cooking time.

lamb and potato curry

Make Lamb Curry (see above). For last 30 minutes of cooking time, add 400-600 ml (2-3 cups) hot water and 400 g (1 lb) potatoes, peeled and cut into quarters.

chicken curry

Serves: 6

Ingredients	Metric	Imperial
Chicken or chicken pieces	1.2 kg	3 lb
Ghee or oil	3 tablespoons	3 tablespoons
Onions, chopped	3 medium	3 medium
Garlic, chopped	3 cloves	3 cloves
Finely grated fresh root ginger	1½ teaspoons	1½ teaspoons
Curry powder	3 tablespoons	3 tablespoons
Chilli powder (optional)	1 teaspoon	1 teaspoon
Salt	3 teaspoons	3 teaspoons
Tomatoes, peeled	3 large	3 large
Chopped fresh coriander or mint	2 tablespoons	2 tablespoons
Garam masala	2 teaspoons	2 teaspoons
Extra chopped fresh coriander or mint (optional)	1 tablespoon	1 tablespoon

Cut chicken into serving pieces. (For curry, the pieces should not be large. Separate drumsticks from thighs. Separate wings from breast. Cut breast in half, or if large, into 4 pieces.)

Heat ghee in a saucepan and gently fry onion, garlic and ginger until soft and golden, stir occasionally. (This will take approximately 20 minutes, depending on thickness of base of pan and how finely the onions have been chopped. Long, slow cooking at this stage is essential for a good curry.)

Add curry powder, chilli powder if used, salt and tomatoes. Add chopped coriander and chicken and stir well to coat chicken pieces with the curry mixture. Cover and simmer for 45 minutes—1 hour, or until chicken is tender. Add garam masala and extra coriander if used, for last 5 minutes of cooking time. Serve with boiled rice or Pilau (see page 13).

Note: Paprika pepper may be substituted for chilli powder for a milder curry with a pleasing red colour.

saffron chicken

Serves: 4

Ingredients	Metric	Imperial
Ghee or oil	3 tablespoons	3 tablespoons
Onion, finely chopped	1 large	1 large
Garlic, finely chopped	3 cloves	3 cloves
Finely grated fresh root ginger	1½ teaspoons	1½ teaspoons
Fresh red chillies, seeded and sliced	3	3
Powdered saffron or saffron strands	good pinch ¼ teaspoon	good pinch ¼ teaspoon
Ground cardamom	½ teaspoon	½ teaspoon
Chicken	800 g	2 lb
Salt	1½ teaspoons	1½ teaspoons

Heat ghee and gently fry onion, garlic, ginger and chillies until onion is soft and starts to turn golden brown. Add saffron and cardamom, stir well, then add chicken, cut into serving pieces. Increase heat and continue to fry, stirring continuously, for 3-4 minutes or until the pieces of chicken are golden and coated with saffron mixture. Add salt, cover and cook over a moderate heat for 10 minutes, or until chicken is tender. Uncover pan and continue to cook until almost all the liquid evaporates.

Serve hot with boiled rice or Parathas (see page 12).

brinjal bartha

Eggplant Purée

Serves: 6

Ingredients	Metric	Imperial
Eggplants	2 large	2 large
Ripe tomatoes	2 large	2 large
Ghee or oil	3 tablespoons	3 tablespoons
Onions, finely chopped	2 medium	2 medium
Finely grated fresh root ginger	1½ teaspoons	1½ teaspoons
Ground turmeric	½ teaspoon	½ teaspoon
Chilli powder (optional)	½ teaspoon	½ teaspoon
Salt	2 teaspoons	2 teaspoons
Garam masala	1 teaspoon	1 teaspoon

Wash and dice eggplants and tomatoes.

Heat ghee in a saucepan and gently fry onion and ginger until they are soft and start to brown. Add turmeric, chilli powder if used, salt and garam masala, mix thoroughly. Add eggplant and tomato, stir well and cover.

Cook gently until vegetables are soft. Stir occasionally to prevent vegetables from sticking to pan. The puree should be fairly thick and dry enough to scoop up with Indian breads. Serve hot or cold.

dhal

Lentil Purée

Serves: 3-4 or 6 as an accompaniment

Ingredients	Metric	Imperial
Red lentils	200 ml	1 cup
Ghee or oil	1½ tablespoons	1½ tablespoons
Onion, finely sliced	1	1
Garlic, finely chopped	2 cloves	2 cloves
Finely chopped fresh root ginger	1 teaspoon	1 teaspoon
Ground turmeric	½ teaspoon	½ teaspoon
Water	600 ml	3 cups
Salt	to taste	to taste

Wash lentils thoroughly, removing those that float on the surface. Drain well. Heat ghee and fry onion, garlic and ginger until onion is golden. Add turmeric and stir well. Add drained lentils and fry for 1-2 minutes. Add water, lower heat, cover and cook for 15 minutes. Add salt, mix thoroughly and continue cooking until lentils are soft and the consistency is thick, similar to porridge.

Serve Dhal plain or garnish with sliced onion, fried until golden brown. Eat with boiled rice, Indian breads, or just by itself.

sukhe alu

Dry Potato Curry

Serves: 3-4 or 6 as an accompaniment

Ingredients	Metric	Imperial
Potatoes	400 g	1 lb
Ghee	1½ tablespoons	1½ tablespoons
Panch phora	1 teaspoon	1 teaspoon
Onion, finely chopped	1 medium	1 medium
Chopped fresh mint or coriander	2 tablespoons	2 tablespoons
Ground turmeric	1 teaspoon	1 teaspoon
Salt	1½ teaspoons	1½ teaspoons
Chilli powder (optional)	½ teaspoon	½ teaspoons
Hot water	50 ml	¼ cup
Garam masala	1 teaspoon	1 teaspoon
Lemon juice	1 tablespoon	1 tablespoon

Peel potatoes, cut into halves and quarters or, if very large, into cubes. Heat ghee in a saucepan and sprinkle in the panch phora. When the seeds start to brown, add onion and fry gently for a few minutes. Add chopped mint, turmeric, salt and chilli powder if used. Add potato, stir well and sprinkle with hot water.

Cover saucepan tightly and cook over a very low heat for 20 minutes, shaking pan occasionally to prevent potatoes from sticking. Sprinkle with garam masala and lemon juice, replace lid and cook for a further 10 minutes.

mixed vegetable bhaji

Spicy Fried Vegetables

Use any combination of vegetables in season. You will find that vegetables cooked in this way are full of flavour. Cook until they are just tender, but still retain their crispness. For a vegetarian meal, serve with rice or Chapatis, Dhal and sambals.

Serves: 4-5 or 6-8 as an accompaniment

Ingredients	Metric	Imperial
Carrots	3 large	3 large
White radishes	2 large	2 large
Green beans	400 g	1 lb
Oil	6 tablespoons	6 tablespoons
Panch phora	2 teaspoons	2 teaspoons
Ground turmeric	1 teaspoon	1 teaspoon
Garlic, chopped	3 cloves	3 cloves
Finely grated fresh root ginger	1½ teaspoons	1½ teaspoons
Salt	1 teaspoon	1 teaspoon

Scrape carrots and radishes, cut into thin slices lengthways, then into strips. String beans and cut into slices diagonally.

Heat oil in a large frying pan or saucepan, add panch phora and turmeric and fry for 1 minute. Add garlic and ginger and continue to fry over a low heat until garlic is golden. Add prepared vegetables and fry, stirring continuously, over a moderate heat for approximately 10 minutes. Add salt, cover and cook for a further 3-4 minutes or until tender but not overcooked. Serve immediately.

cauliflower bhaji

Proceed as for Mixed Vegetable Bhaji (see above), but substitute half a head of cauliflower for the carrots, white radishes and green beans. Separate cauliflower into flowerettes and cut in slices, making sure some of the stalk is attached to each piece. Sprinkle Cauliflower Bhaji with 1 teaspoon of garam masala towards end of cooking time.

podina chatni

Ground Mint Chutney

Ingredients	Metric	Imperial
Fresh mint leaves	200 ml (firmly packed)	1 cup (firmly packed)
Shallots	8	8
Fresh green chillies	2	2
Garlic (optional)	1 clove	1 clove
Salt	1 teaspoon	1 teaspoon
Sugar	2 teaspoons	2 teaspoons
Garam masala	1 teaspoon	1 teaspoon
Lemon juice	4 tablespoons	4 tablespoons
Water	2 tablespoons	2 tablespoons

Finely chop the mint and shallots. Seed chillies and chop very finely. Crush garlic with salt. Combine prepared ingredients and crush with a mortar and pestle. Add remaining ingredients and mix well.

Alternatively, place all the ingredients in an electric blender container, cover and blend on high speed until smooth.

Pack into a small dish, smooth the surface, cover and chill until ready to serve.

dhania chatni

Fresh Coriander Chutney

Proceed as for Podina Chatni, (see above) but replace the mint with an equal quantity of fresh coriander. A teaspoonful of chopped fresh root ginger may also be added if desired.

Note: A medium sized onion may be substituted for the shallots in both recipes.

cucumber salad

Serves: 4-6

Ingredients	Metric	Imperial
Green cucumbers	2 large	2 large
Salt	2 teaspoons	2 teaspoons
Garlic, crushed	1 clove	1 clove
Finely grated fresh root ginger	1 teaspoon	1 teaspoon
Sour cream	200 ml	1 cup

Peel cucumbers and slice very thinly. Place in a bowl and sprinkle with salt. Chill in refrigerator for approximately 1 hour. Pour off the liquid that collects and drain well. Mix garlic, ginger and sour cream together, add cucumber and mix thoroughly. Cover and chill until ready to serve.

1 ras gulas
2 singaras
3 pakoras
4 samoosas
5 nan khatai
6 falooda

crab curry

cucumber raita

Dice or grate 2 peeled cucumbers. Sprinkle with 2 teaspoons of salt and chill for approximately 1 hour. Pour off liquid and drain thoroughly. Mix with 200 ml (1 cup) natural yoghurt. Season to taste with salt, garam masala and chilli powder.

tomato and mint salad

Serves: 4-6

Ingredients	Metric	Imperial
Firm red tomatoes, peeled and diced	3	3
Chopped fresh mint	3 tablespoons	3 tablespoons
Lemon juice	2 tablespoons	2 tablespoons
Salt	to taste	to taste

Combine all ingredients, cover and chill until ready to serve.

onion sambal

Ingredients	Metric	Imperial
Onions, finely sliced	2 medium	2 medium
Lemon juice	1 tablespoon	1 tablespoon
Chilli powder	½ teaspoon	½ teaspoon
Salt	½ teaspoon	½ teaspoon

Sprinkle onion with lemon juice, chilli powder and salt and toss together lightly until thoroughly mixed. Serve as an accompaniment to Lamb Kebabs (see page 18) and Parathas (see page 12) or curries and rice.

samoosas

Small Savoury Pastries
These are a savoury served for afternoon tea in India, but they are equally suitable to serve with pre-dinner drinks.

Yield: 32-36

Ingredients	Metric	Imperial
Pastry:		
Plain flour	300 ml	1½ cups
Salt	¾ teaspoon	¾ teaspoon
Oil or ghee	1 tablespoon	1 tablespoon
Warm water	approximately 100 ml	approximately ½ cup
Filling:		
Oil or ghee	1 tablespoon	1 tablespoon
Garlic, finely chopped	1 clove	1 clove
Finely chopped fresh root ginger	1 teaspoon	1 teaspoon
Onions, finely chopped	2 medium	2 medium
Curry powder	2 teaspoons	2 teaspoons
Salt	½ teaspoon	½ teaspoon
Vinegar or lemon juice	1 tablespoon	1 tablespoon
Minced steak	200 g	8 oz
Hot water	100 ml	½ cup
Garam masala	1 teaspoon	1 teaspoon
Chopped fresh coriander or mint	2 tablespoons	2 tablespoons
Oil	for frying	for frying

Pastry: Sieve flour and salt into a mixing bowl, add oil and warm water and mix thoroughly until ingredients are combined. (Add a little more water if necessary to combine ingredients.) Knead for approximately 10 minutes or until dough is elastic. Cover with clear plastic and set aside while preparing filling.

Filling: Heat ghee in a saucepan and fry garlic, ginger and half the onion until onion is soft. Add curry powder, salt and vinegar, mix well. Add minced steak and fry over a high heat, stirring continuously until meat changes colour. Turn heat down and add hot water. Cover pan and cook until meat is tender and all the liquid has been absorbed.

Towards end of cooking time, stir frequently to prevent meat from sticking to base of pan. Sprinkle with garam masala and chopped coriander, remove from heat and allow to cool. Mix in reserved chopped onion.

Take small pieces of dough, form into balls and on a lightly floured board, roll each one thinly to a circle, (the size of a saucer). Cut each circle in half. Place a teaspoon of filling on one side of each half circle and brush edges with water. Fold dough over and press edges together firmly. You will now have triangular shaped Samoosas.

When they are all made, heat oil in a deep pan and fry a few at a time until golden brown on both sides. Drain on absorbent paper and serve hot.

singaras

Savoury pastries similar to Samoosas.

Proceed as for Samoosas (see page 26), but substitute a filling of spiced potatoes. Boil, peel and dice 2 large potatoes. Cool, then sprinkle with ½ teaspoon chilli powder, ½ teaspoon panch phora, 1 teaspoon ground cummin and 1 teaspoon salt. Add 2 tablespoons lemon juice and mix together thoroughly.

Note: Samoosas and Singaras may also be made using spring roll wrapers (available from some Chinese stores). Cut into 6 cm (2½-inch) strips the length of the sheet of pastry. Place a teaspoonful of filling at one end and fold the pastry over diagonally, then fold again and again, still keeping a triangular shape. Moisten end of strip with water or egg white and press lightly. Fry as above.

pakorhas

Savoury Vegetable Fritters

Served in India as a tea time savoury. Try them as an accompaniment to a meal instead of plain cooked vegetables, or serve as a party savoury.

Use small pieces of raw potato, onion, cauliflower, eggplant, zucchini and green capsicum or a combination of your own choice.

Yield: 10-12

Ingredients	Metric	Imperial
Besan (lentil flour)	300 ml	1½ cups
Garam masala	1 teaspoon	1 teaspoon
Salt	2 teaspoons	2 teaspoons
Ground turmeric	½ teaspoon	½ teaspoon
Chilli powder (optional)	½ teaspoon	½ teaspoon
Water	scant 200 ml	scant 1 cup
Garlic, crushed or	1 clove	1 clove
garlic powder	½ teaspoon	½ teaspoon
Mixed chopped vegetables	800 ml	4 cups
Oil	for deep frying	for deep frying

Sieve besan, garam masala, salt, turmeric and chilli powder if used into a mixing bowl. Add water gradually, mixing ingredients to a thick batter. Stir in garlic and beat thoroughly. Allow batter to stand for 30 minutes, then beat again.

Add chopped vegetables to batter and mix thoroughly.

Heat oil in a deep pan. Drop teaspoons of mixture into the oil and fry over a moderate heat until pale gold on both sides, lift out of oil with a slotted spoon and drain on absorbent paper.

Just before serving, heat oil again. When almost smoking hot, return Pakorhas to the pan, a few at a time, for approximately 30 seconds or until golden brown on both sides. (The second frying makes them very crisp.) Drain on absorbent paper and serve immediately.

<u>Note:</u> If you prefer to lighten the batter and lessen the strong lentil flour flavour, use half lentil flour and half self-raising flour—a little liberty that results in puffier Pakorhas and won't topple the Taj Mahal!

ras gulas

One of the most popular Indian sweetmeats, Ras Gulas means, literally, balls of juice. Walnut-size balls of home-made cream cheese are simmered in sugar syrup with added exotic flavours.

Serves: 5-6

Ingredients	Metric	Imperial
Milk	1.5 litres	3 pints
Lemon juice, strained	3-4 tablespoons	3-4 tablespoons
Fine semolina	2 teaspoons	2 teaspoons
Sugar cubes	10	10
Sugar	400 ml	2 cups
Water	800 ml	4 cups
Cardamom pods	8	8
Rose water	2 tablespoons	2 tablespoons

Pour milk into a large saucepan and bring almost to boiling point. As milk starts to rise in pan, remove from heat, add slightly warmed lemon juice and stir once. Allow mixture to stand for 5 minutes, when solid lumps will have formed. If milk does not curdle (lemons vary in acid content) reheat milk and add more lemon juice. Pour into a large colander lined with a large square of clean muslin. Drain for 30 minutes or until all the whey has dripped out, or place muslin-wrapped curds on a plate and press with another plate to remove as much liquid as possible.

Turn curds out on a marble slab or laminated surface. Knead for 5 minutes, using the heel of the hand. Add semolina and knead again until the cream cheese is smooth. When the palm of the hand becomes greasy, the cheese is ready for moulding. Form into 10 walnut-size balls, moulding each one around a cube of sugar.

In a large saucepan, heat sugar and water together until sugar dissolves, then bring to the boil and simmer 5 minutes. Pour half the syrup into a jug and set aside. Place Ras Gulas and bruised cardamom pods in the syrup in the saucepan and bring to the boil. Simmer over a very low heat, uncovered, until the balls swell and become spongy, approximately 1 hour. Occasionally add a little reserved sugar syrup to prevent syrup in pan from becoming too thick.

Allow to cool until lukewarm, then add rose water. Serve warm or at room temperature, one or two Ras Gulas to a serving.

<u>Note:</u> Do not serve chilled as the Ras Gulas become firm and it is essential they should retain their spongy texture.

nan khatai

Crisp Semolina Shortbread

These little shortbread biscuits made with ghee have a delightful melting texture.
Yield: approximately 24
Cooking time: approximately 30 minutes
Oven temperature: 150-160 C (300-325 F)

Ingredients	Metric	Imperial
Ghee	100 g	4 oz
Sugar	100 ml	½ cup
Fine semolina	200 ml	1 cup
Plain flour	50 ml	¼ cup
Ground cardamom	1 teaspoon	1 teaspoon

Cream ghee and sugar together until light. Add the sieved semolina, flour and cardamom, mix well. Allow mixture to stand for 30 minutes.

Take a scant tablespoon of the mixture, roll into a ball, then flatten slightly and place on an ungreased baking tray. Repeat process with remaining mixture, leaving a little space between biscuits.

Bake in a slow oven until biscuits are pale golden, approximately 30 minutes. Cool on a wire cooling tray. Store in an air-tight container.

ceylon

I was born on this small, beautiful tropical island with its extremes of climate and contrasts in scenery.

Within less than 100 miles you can travel from golden beaches and coconut palms to hills where, 6,000 feet above sea level, the air is cool and crisp and the natural vegetation includes conifers and pines. Here, English and Scottish planters grow the best tea in the world and feel at home in the cold, misty climate while on the coastal plains there is a year-round temperature of 90°F and city dwellers seek the comfort of air-conditioned buildings.

In spite of its tiny size, Ceylon boasts an amazing variety in food. While the island has a rich heritage of indigenous dishes, some of those brought there by other races are now considered Ceylonese too. It does not matter that years ago this or that style of eating was introduced by foreigners who came and stayed, either as traders or conquerors—among them Indians, Arabs, Malays, Moors, Portuguese, Dutch and British. Though Ceylon does not grow enough rice to be self-supporting, rice is the staple food. When enquiring whether one has had a meal, the literal translation of the question as asked in the Sinhalese language is, 'Have you eaten rice?' And all over Ceylon the midday meal is rice and curry, Sinhalese style.

For such a meal everything is put on the table at once—rice, fish and meat curries, coconut soup, vegetables and accompaniments. It is perfectly correct to have a serving of everything on your plate at one time.

Soup may be ladled over the rice or sipped from a cup.

Each morning before they start to cook, the women must grind their spices and seasonings. This is done on an oblong stone the size of a small pillow, using another stone shaped like a bolster. Primitive, but it is standard equipment in every home.

In Ceylonese curries, the spices are dark-roasted, giving them an aroma and flavour completely different from Indian curries. So when making a Ceylon curry be sure the label says, 'Ceylon curry powder'.

In Ceylon, as in any other country, the most typical food is cooked in the villages but getting precise recipes is almost impossible. They don't cook by a book. A pinch of this, a handful of that, a good swirl of salty water. Taste, consider, adjust seasoning—that's the way Sinhalese women cook, and no two women cook exactly alike.

Even using the same ingredients, the interpretation of a recipe is completely individual.

Ask a cook how much of a certain ingredient she used and she'll say, 'This much' showing you with her hand. Spoon measures would be looked upon as an affectation. You watch, make notes and try to achieve the same results by trial and error. And when you arrive at the correct formula, write it down for posterity!

rotis

Similar to the Indian flat breads, but this Ceylon version contains fresh grated coconut or, in its absence, desiccated coconut. Serve with curries and sambols. It is a popular breakfast in Ceylon.

Yield: 6-8

Ingredients	Metric	Imperial
Self-raising, roti or rice flour	400 ml	2 cups
Desiccated coconut	100 ml	½ cup
Salt	1 teaspoon	1 teaspoon
Water	scant 200 ml	scant 1 cup
Ghee or oil	for cooking	for cooking

Mix flour, coconut and salt in a mixing bowl. Add enough water to form a soft dough. Knead dough until it forms a ball and does not stick to sides of the bowl. Rest dough for approximately 30 minutes.

Shape dough into balls, approximately the size of a golf ball. Pat each one out to a circle the size of a saucer. Cook on a hot griddle or in a heavy frying pan, very lightly greased with ghee or oil. Serve hot.

kiri bath

Milk Rice

A simple preparation of rice cooked in coconut milk, Kiri Bath is one of the traditions of the Sinhalese people. It is a 'must' on New Year's Day, and on the first day of each month it is the accepted breakfast dish. It is usually served with hot sambols, but some prefer it with grated jaggery or palm sugar. If you have difficulty in buying jaggery, use unrefined black sugar as a substitute. (Available at health food stores.)

Serves: 4-5

Ingredients	Metric	Imperial
White short grain rice	400 ml	2 cups
Water	600 ml	3 cups
Thick Coconut Milk (see page 66)	400 ml	2 cups
Salt	2 teaspoons	2 teaspoons
Cinnamon stick (optional)	1	1

Place rice and water in a saucepan and bring to the boil. Cover and cook for 15 minutes. Add coconut milk, salt and cinnamon, stir well with the handle of a wooden spoon. Cover pan and cook over a low heat for a further 10-15 minutes, when all the milk will be absorbed. Remove cinnamon stick. Cool slightly. Turn out on to a flat serving plate. Cut into large diamond shapes and serve with Pol Sambola (see page 43).

kaha bath

Yellow Rice

A special occasion dish, in which the rice is cooked in coconut milk and delicately flavoured with spices.

Serves: 6-8

Ingredients	Metric	Imperial
Long grain rice	600 ml	3 cups
Coconut Milk (see page 66)	approximately 1 litre	approximately 5 cups
Ghee	4 tablespoons	4 tablespoons
Onions, finely sliced	2 medium	2 medium
Cloves	6	6
Peppercorns	20	20
Cardamom pods, bruised	12	12
Ground turmeric	1½ teaspoons	1½ teaspoons
Salt	3½ teaspoons	3½ teaspoons
Curry leaves	12	12
Dried lemon grass	6 strips	6 strips
Dried rampé leaf	4 pieces	4 pieces

Wash rice and drain thoroughly.

Heat ghee in a large saucepan, add onion and fry until it begins to turn golden brown. Add cloves, peppercorns, cardamom pods, turmeric, salt, curry leaves, lemon grass and rampé leaf. Add rice and fry, stirring continuously, for 2-3 minutes, until the rice is well coated with ghee and turmeric. Add coconut milk and bring to the boil. Lower heat, cover and cook for 20-25 minutes without lifting lid.

When rice is cooked, the spices will have come to the top. Remove spices and leaves used for flavouring and fluff up rice lightly with a fork. Serve hot, accompanied by Pork Badun (see page 40), Brinjal Pahi (see page 46), Chilli Sambol (see page 44) and Cucumber Sambol (see page 45).

ghee rice

A simple version of the Indian pilau.

Serves: 4-5

Ingredients	Metric	Imperial
Basmati or other long grain rice	400 ml	2 cups
Ghee	2½ tablespoons	2½ tablespoons
Onion, finely sliced	1 large	1 large
Cloves	4	4
Cardamom pods, bruised	6	6
Cinnamon stick	8 cm piece	3-inch piece
Hot beef, chicken or mutton stock or water and stock cubes	700 ml	3½ cups
Salt	2½ teaspoons	2½ teaspoons

Wash rice well and drain for at least 30 minutes. Heat ghee in a saucepan and fry onion until golden, add spices and drained rice. Fry, stirring with slotted metal spoon, for 5 minutes over a moderate heat. Add hot stock and salt and bring to the boil.

Reduce heat to very low, cover pan tightly with lid and cook for 15-20 minutes without lifting lid. At end of cooking time, uncover and allow steam to escape, stand for 5 minutes. Gently fluff up rice with fork, removing whole spices.

When transferring rice to a serving dish, again use a slotted metal spoon to avoid crushing grains of rice. Serve hot, accompanied by curries of meat and vegetables, pickles and sambols.

lampries

Serves: 16-18
Cooking time: approximately 20-25 minutes
Oven temperature: 170-190°C (350-375°F)

Just as biriani is the ultimate in festive meals in India, Lampries is the 'special occasion' dish in Ceylon. If you are invited to a meal in a Ceylonese home and Lampries are served, you are being honoured.

The name is from the Dutch word, Lomprijst, and it is a fascinating combination of rice cooked in stock, Dutch-style forcemeat balls, Sinhalese curries and sambols, all wrapped in banana leaves and baked. Use large, wide banana leaves, strip them from the centre rib and cut into pieces, approximately 30-38 cm (12-15-inches) long. Wash, dry with a clean cloth and heat over a gas flame for a few seconds on each side. This makes them pliable and they will fold without splitting. If you cook by electricity, put banana leaves in a large basin or sink and pour boiling water over. If no banana leaves are available, use 38 cm (15-inch) squares of aluminium foil.
Prepare Ghee Rice (see page 34) making three times the quantity. For 1.2 litres (6 cups) rice use 1.9 litres (9½ cups) stock. On each piece of leaf or aluminium foil, place 200 ml (1 cup) firmly packed Ghee Rice. Around rice arrange 2 tablespoons Lampries Curry (see page 36); 2 Frikkadels (see page 42); 2 teaspoons Brinjal Pahi (see page 46); 1 teaspoon Chilli Sambol (see page 44) and 1 heaping teaspoon Prawn Blachan (see page 47). Pour 2 tablespoons thick Coconut Milk (see page 66) over the rice.

Fold leaf over and fasten with bamboo skewers (obtainable from barbecue departments of large stores) or fold aluminium foil over to make a neat oblong package. Some people prefer to enclose leaf parcels in aluminium foil. (This is a good idea in case the leaf splits while heating or serving.)
Heat Lampries in a moderate oven for approximately 20-25 minutes. Arrange on a large tray.

When guests open the Lampries, the fragrance of the food is unbelievably appetizing. Allow two lampries for each man and one for each woman. A bowl of chilled Cucumber Sambol (see page 45) is served as an accompaniment.

<u>Note:</u> It is practical to make a large number of Lampries as they are ideal for parties. They freeze well and may be kept frozen for two months. Heat in a moderate oven 170-190°C (350-375°F) from frozen state for 40 minutes or 20 minutes if first thawed to room temperature.

lampries curry

This curry, traditionally included in Lampries (see page 35), is made with four different meats and is delicious and unusual.

Serves: 16-18

Ingredients	Metric	Imperial
Chuck steak	400 g	1 lb
Mutton	400 g	1 lb
Salt	5 teaspoons	5 teaspoons
Cardamom pods	8	8
Peppercorns	20	20
Chicken pieces, breasts or thighs	400 g	1 lb
Pork shoulder	400 g	1 lb
Ghee	1 tablespoon	1 tablespoon
Oil	2 tablespoons	2 tablespoons
Onions, finely chopped	4 medium	4 medium
Garlic, finely chopped	8 cloves	8 cloves
Finely chopped fresh root ginger	1 tablespoon	1 tablespoon
Ground curry leaves	2 teaspoons	2 teaspoons
Fenugreek seeds (optional)	¼ teaspoon	¼ teaspoon
Ceylon curry powder	4 tablespoons	4 tablespoons
Ground turmeric	1 teaspoon	1 teaspoon
Chilli powder	2 teaspoons	2 teaspoons
Cinnamon stick	8 cm piece	3-inch piece
Ground cardamom	1 teaspoon	1 teaspoon
Dried rampé leaf (optional)	6-8 pieces	6-8 pieces
Dried lemon grass (optional)	12 strips	12 strips
Lemon juice	2 tablespoons	2 tablespoons
Coconut Milk (see page 66)	1 litre	5 cups
Extra salt	to taste	to taste

Place steak and mutton in a large saucepan. Cover with cold water, add 2 teaspoons of the salt, cardamom pods and peppercorns. Cover pan and simmer for 30 minutes. Add chicken pieces and simmer for a further 15 minutes. Allow to cool slightly, strain, and reserve stock for boiling rice. Cut pork and parboiled meats into very small dice.

Heat ghee and oil in a large saucepan and gently fry onion, garlic, ginger and curry leaves until onion is soft and starts to turn golden. Add fenugreek seeds if used and fry 1 minute longer. Add curry powder, turmeric, chilli powder, cinnamon stick, cardamom, rampé leaf and lemon grass if used. Add remaining 3 teaspoons salt, lemon juice, diced pork and half the coconut milk. Stir well. Cover and cook over a low heat for 30 minutes, stirring occasionally. Add parboiled meats and remaining coconut milk, cover and simmer for approximately 1½ hours, or until meat is tender and gravy is reduced. Add extra salt to taste if necessary. Remove cinnamon stick, rampé leaf and lemon grass before serving.

crab curry

A favourite in Ceylon where crabs are plentiful and cheap, and are always sold live. Cooked crabs may be used. They are a lot easier — and safer — to handle.

Serves: 4-6

Ingredients	Metric	Imperial
Crabs	2 large	2 large
Onions, finely chopped	3 medium	3 medium
Garlic, finely chopped	6 cloves	6 cloves
Finely grated fresh root ginger	2 teaspoons	2 teaspoons
Fenugreek seeds	½ teaspoon	½ teaspoon
Curry leaves	10	10
Cinnamon stick	8 cm piece	3-inch piece
Chilli powder	1-2 teaspoons	1-2 teaspoons
Ground turmeric	1 teaspoon	1 teaspoon
Salt	3 teaspoons	3 teaspoons
Thin Coconut Milk (see page 66)	800 ml	4 cups
Desiccated coconut	2 tablespoons	2 tablespoons
Ground rice	1 tablespoon	1 tablespoon
Thick Coconut Milk (see page 66)	400 ml	2 cups
Lemon juice	3 tablespoons	3 tablespoons

Remove large shells of crabs and discard fibrous tissue found under the shell. Divide each crab into 4 portions, breaking each body in half and separating large claws from body. Leave legs attached to body.

Place onion, garlic, ginger, fenugreek seeds, curry leaves, cinnamon stick, chilli powder, turmeric, salt and thin coconut milk into a large saucepan. Cover and simmer gently for 30 minutes. Add crabs and cook for a further 20 minutes. If pan is not large enough, add half the pieces of crab at a time and simmer each batch for 20 minutes. (The pieces of crab should be submerged in the sauce while cooking.)

Heat desiccated coconut and ground rice separately in a dry frying pan over a moderate heat, stirring constantly to prevent burning, until each is golden brown. Place in an electric blender container, add half the thick coconut milk, cover and blend on high speed for 1 minute. Add to curry with lemon juice. Wash out blender with remaining coconut milk, add to pan and simmer, uncovered, for a further 10 minutes.

Serve with boiled white rice.

Note: Onions vary so much in different countries and even from one season to the next. If they are inclined to be large and tough, first soften by cooking gently in 2-3 tablespoons oil about 20 minutes before including in recipe.

prawn coconut curry

Serves: 8

Proceed as for Crab Curry (see above), but substitute 1 kg (2½ lb) large raw prawns for crabs. Shell and de-vein prawns.

Add prawns to coconut gravy and simmer for 15-20 minutes. After adding coconut and ground rice mixture and lemon juice, simmer 1-2 minutes longer. Serve with boiled white rice.

fish curry

Serves: 4-6

Ingredients	Metric	Imperial
Jewfish, kingfish or cod steaks	4 large	4 large
Ground black pepper	1 teaspoon	1 teaspoon
Salt	1 teaspoon	1 teaspoon
Ground turmeric	1 teaspoon	1 teaspoon
Oil	for frying	for frying
Gravy:		
Oil	2 tablespoons	2 tablespoons
Onions, finely chopped	2 medium	2 medium
Fenugreek seeds	¼ teaspoon	¼ teaspoon
Garlic, finely sliced	2 cloves	2 cloves
Finely chopped fresh root ginger	1 teaspoon	1 teaspoon
Cinnamon stick	1 small	1 small
Dried rampé leaf	4 pieces	4 pieces
Curry leaves or	8	8
ground curry leaves	½ teaspoon	½ teaspoon
Ceylon curry powder	1½ tablespoons	1½ tablespoons
Tamarind liquid	50 ml	¼ cup
Coconut Milk (see page 66)	400 ml	2 cups
Salt	to taste	to taste

Wash fish steaks, dry with absorbent paper and rub well with combined pepper, salt and turmeric. Heat approximately 1 cm (½-inch) oil in a large frying pan and fry fish quickly on both sides until golden. Drain on absorbent paper while preparing the gravy.

Gravy: Heat oil in a large saucepan and gently fry onion, fenugreek seeds, garlic and ginger until onion is soft and golden. Add cinnamon stick, rampé and curry leaves and curry powder, fry for 2 minutes, stirring continuously. Mix in tamarind liquid and coconut milk and simmer, uncovered, until gravy is thickened and slightly reduced. Add salt to taste.

Place fish steaks in gravy. (If too large, divide each one in half.) Spoon gravy over fish and simmer for approximately 10 minutes. Serve hot with boiled rice and vegetable curries.

omelet curry

Serves: 4

Prepare gravy as for Fish Curry (see above). Beat 6 eggs together, add 1 finely chopped small onion, 1 seeded and finely chopped fresh chilli, 2 teaspoons chopped fresh dill (or ½ teaspoon dried dill weed) and salt and pepper to taste. Heat a little butter in a frying pan and make 2 omelets with mixture. Cut each omelet in 3 pieces. Heat through in prepared gravy and serve with boiled rice and accompaniments.

Variation: Proceed as for Vegetable Curry (see page 41) but substitute pieces of omelet for mixed vegetables. Serve with boiled rice and accompaniments.

beef smoore

A large piece of beef, cooked in a spicy coconut milk mixture, cut in slices like roast beef and served with plenty of the rich, thick gravy spooned over. Accompany with boiled rice or Rotis (see page 32) and Onion Sambal (see page 25).

Serves: 6-8

Ingredients	Metric	Imperial
Blade or chuck steak	1.2 kg	3 lb
Onions, finely chopped	2 medium	2 medium
Garlic, finely chopped	6 cloves	6 cloves
Finely chopped fresh root ginger	1 tablespoon	1 tablespoon
Cinnamon stick	8 cm piece	3-inch piece
Curry leaves	10	10
Dried lemon grass	6 strips	6 strips
Ceylon curry powder	3 tablespoons	3 tablespoons
Fenugreek seeds	½ teaspoon	½ teaspoon
Vinegar	100 ml	½ cup
Pickled lime or	½ lime	½ lime
tamarind liquid	100 ml	½ cup
Thin Coconut Milk (see page 66)	600 ml	3 cups
Ground turmeric	1 teaspoon	1 teaspoon
Chilli powder	2 teaspoons	2 teaspoons
Salt	2 teaspoons or to taste	2 teaspoons or to taste
Thick Coconut Milk (see page 66)	200 ml	1 cup
Ghee	2½ tablespoons	2½ tablespoons

Pierce the meat well with a skewer and place in a large saucepan with all the ingredients except thick coconut milk and ghee. Cover and simmer gently until the meat is tender, approximately 1½-2 hours. Add thick coconut milk and cook, uncovered, 15 minutes longer.

Lift meat out on to a serving dish and if gravy is too thin, reduce by boiling rapidly, uncovered. Transfer gravy to a bowl. Rinse pan to remove any gravy, return to stove and heat ghee in it. Fry meat on all sides, pour gravy over meat and heat through.

pork badun

Fried Pork Curry

Serves: 6-8

Ingredients	Metric	Imperial
Pork	800 g	2 lb
Oil	3 tablespoons	3 tablespoons
Curry leaves	10	10
Fenugreek seeds (optional)	¼ teaspoon	¼ teaspoon
Onions, finely chopped	2 medium	2 medium
Garlic, finely chopped	4 cloves	4 cloves
Finely grated fresh root ginger	1½ teaspoons	1½ teaspoons
Ceylon curry powder	3 tablespoons	3 tablespoons
Chilli powder	1-2 teaspoons	1-2 teaspoons
Salt	2 teaspoons	2 teaspoons
Vinegar	1 tablespoon	1 tablespoon
Tamarind pulp	1 tablespoon	1 tablespoon
Hot water	300 ml	1½ cups
Cinnamon stick	5 cm piece	2-inch piece
Cardamom pods	4	4
Thick Coconut Milk (see page 66)	200 ml	1 cup

Cut pork into large cubes. Heat oil in a large saucepan and fry curry leaves and fenugreek seeds if used until they start to brown, add onion and garlic and fry over a low heat until onion is soft and golden. Add ginger, curry powder, chilli powder, salt, vinegar and pork. Fry over a high heat, stirring thoroughly until meat is well coated with the spice mixture. Squeeze tamarind pulp in hot water, strain and discard seeds. Add tamarind liquid, cinnamon stick and cardamom pods to pan, cover and cook over a low heat until pork is tender, approximately 1 hour. Add coconut milk and cook 10 minutes longer, uncovered.

Pour off gravy into another saucepan, return pork to heat and allow to fry in its own fat. (If pork is not fat enough, add 1 tablespoon ghee or oil to pan.) When pork is nicely browned, return gravy to pan and cook, uncovered, until gravy is heated through and thick.

Serve hot with boiled rice, Vegetable Curry (see page 41), Brinjal Pahi (see page 46), Pol Sambola (see page 43) and Cucumber Sambol (see page 45).

1 kaha bath
2 pork badun
3 cashew nut curry
4 fried eggplant sambol
5 pappadams
6 fried sprats
7 pol sambola

1 chah-zan
2 panthé kowshwé
3 fried chillies
4 roasted chick peas
5 fried garlic
6 chilli powder
7 sliced shallots
8 lemon segments

vegetable curry

Here is the basic 'white' curry. In it you can cook beans, pumpkin, okra, capsicums, potatoes, zucchini, asparagus or other vegetables of your choice.

Serves: 4-6

Ingredients	Metric	Imperial
Thin Coconut Milk (see page 66)	600 ml	3 cups
Onion, finely sliced	1 medium	1 medium
Fresh chillies, seeded and split	2	2
Ground turmeric	½ teaspoon	½ teaspoon
Garlic, finely sliced	2 cloves	2 cloves
Finely grated fresh root ginger	½ teaspoon	½ teaspoon
Cinnamon stick	5 cm piece	2-inch piece
Dried rampé leaf	4 pieces	4 pieces
Dried lemon grass	4 strips	4 strips
Curry leaves	8	8
Vegetables, sliced	600 g	1½ lb
Salt	to taste	to taste
Thick Coconut Milk (see page 66)	200 ml	1 cup

Place all ingredients, except sliced mixed vegetables, salt and thick coconut milk, in a large saucepan and simmer gently, uncovered, for approximately 10 minutes. Add sliced vegetables and salt and cook gently until vegetables are just tender. Add thick coconut milk and simmer approximately 5 minutes longer.

Serve with boiled rice, other curries and accompaniments.

cashew nut curry

A curry of fresh cashew nuts is one of the delights of Sinhalese cooking. Fresh cashew nuts are not obtainable except in the country in which they are grown, but raw cashew nuts, available from health food shops and Chinese grocery stores, make a very good substitute if soaked overnight in cold water.

Proceed as for Vegetable Curry (see above), but substitute 200 g (8 oz) raw cashew nuts for sliced vegetables. Simmer for approximately 30 minutes, or until cashew nuts are tender. Serve with boiled rice and other accompaniments.

frikkadels

Dutch Forcemeat Balls

Yield: approximately 40

Ingredients	Metric	Imperial
Butter	1 tablespoon	1 tablespoon
Onion, finely chopped	1 small	1 small
Minced steak	400 g	1 lb
Soft white breadcrumbs	100 ml	½ cup
Salt	1½ teaspoons	1½ teaspoons
Ground black pepper	½ teaspoon	½ teaspoon
Chopped fresh dill or dried dill weed	2 teaspoons ½ teaspoon	2 teaspoons ½ teaspoon
Ground cinnamon	¼ teaspoon	¼ teaspoon
Ground cloves	¼ teaspoon	¼ teaspoon
Garlic, crushed	1 clove	1 clove
Finely grated fresh root ginger	½ teaspoon	½ teaspoon
Worcestershire sauce or lemon juice	2 teaspoons	2 teaspoons
Egg, beaten	1	1
Dry breadcrumbs	for coating	for coating
Oil or ghee	for deep frying	for deep frying

Heat butter in a small frying pan and gently fry onion until soft. Combine with minced steak, breadcrumbs, salt, pepper, chopped dill, cinnamon, cloves, garlic, ginger and Worcestershire sauce. Mix thoroughly and form into small balls, (approximately 2.5 cm (1-inch) in diameter.) Dip into beaten egg and coat with dry breadcrumbs. Deep fry in hot oil until golden brown. Drain on absorbent paper before serving.

pol sambola

Coconut Sambol

Ingredients	Metric	Imperial
Desiccated coconut	200 ml	1 cup
Salt	1 teaspoon	1 teaspoon
Chilli powder	1 teaspoon or to taste	1 teaspoon or to taste
Paprika pepper	2 teaspoons	2 teaspoons
Maldive fish or prawn powder (optional)	2 teaspoons	2 teaspoons
Lemon juice	2 tablespoons or to taste	2 tablespoons or to taste
Onion, finely chopped	1 medium	1 medium
Hot milk	2-3 tablespoons	2-3 tablespoons

Combine desiccated coconut, salt, chilli powder, paprika pepper and maldive fish if used, in a bowl. Sprinkle with lemon juice, onion and milk. Mix well with the hand, rubbing the ingredients together so that the coconut is evenly moistened. Pile into a small bowl.

Note: If liked, add 1-2 fresh red or green chillies, seeded and finely chopped.

kalupol sambola

Roasted Coconut Sambol

In Ceylon, this is made with fresh coconut, roasted in the ashes of a fire until dark brown, then ground on a large stone, but this adaptation is a lot easier to make.

Ingredients	Metric	Imperial
Desiccated coconut	200 ml	1 cup
Onions, finely chopped	2 medium	2 medium
Salt	1 teaspoon	1 teaspoon
Maldive fish or prawn powder	2 teaspoons	2 teaspoons
Lemon juice	approximately 50 ml	approximately ¼ cup

Heat desiccated coconut in a heavy based frying pan and stir constantly until it is evenly browned. (It should be a fairly deep brown, but be careful not to burn.) Spread coconut on a large plate to cool.

Combine all ingredients in an electric blender container, cover and blend on high speed until a smooth paste is formed. (It may be necessary to add a little more chopped onion or lemon juice if there is not sufficient liquid.)

Shape into a round flat cake and mark the top in a criss-cross pattern with a fork or the back of a knife. Serve with rice and curry.

chilli sambol

Chilli sambol is a popular accompaniment to rice and curry. Thanks to convenient canned 'prawns in spices' (sold in Chinese food stores) this simplified version can be prepared in a fraction of the time and tastes as good as the original recipe.

Ingredients	Metric	Imperial
Oil	100 ml	½ cup
Onions, finely sliced	4 medium	4 medium
Chilli powder	2 teaspoons	2 teaspoons
Prawns in spices	1 x 170 g can	1 x 6 oz can
Vinegar	2 tablespoons	2 tablespoons
Salt	to taste	to taste
Sugar	2 teaspoons	2 teaspoons

Heat oil in a large frying pan and fry onion very slowly, stirring occasionally, until soft and transparent. (It is important to fry onions slowly —all the liquid in the onion must evaporate if the sambol is to have good keeping qualities.)

When the onion is golden brown, add chilli powder, prawns in spices and vinegar. Stir thoroughly, cover and simmer for 10 minutes. Uncover pan and continue simmering, stirring occasionally, until liquid evaporates and oil starts to separate from other ingredients. Season to taste with salt. Remove from heat, stir in sugar and allow to cool before placing in a clean dry jar. Use in small quantities.

Note: If a hotter sambol is preferred, increase quantity of chilli powder.

fried onion sambol

Ingredients	Metric	Imperial
Oil	100 ml	½ cup
Onions, finely sliced	2 large	2 large
Dried chillies, broken into pieces	6	6
Maldive fish or prawn powder	2 tablespoons	2 tablespoons
Salt	1 teaspoon or to taste	1 teaspoon or to taste
Lemon juice	2 tablespoons	2 tablespoons

Heat oil in a frying pan and fry onion slowly until soft and transparent. Add chillies and maldive fish, cover and cook for 10-15 minutes, or until oil separates from other ingredients. Stir occasionally while cooking. Add salt and lemon juice and cook a few minutes longer. Serve with boiled rice and curries.

cucumber sambol

Ingredients	Metric	Imperial
Green cucumber	1 large or 2 small	1 large or 2 small
Salt	2 teaspoons	2 teaspoons
Thick Coconut Milk (see page 66)	100 ml	½ cup
Fresh red chilli, seeded and sliced	1	1
Fresh green chilli, seeded and sliced	1	1
Onion, cut in paper thin slices	1 small	1 small
Lemon juice	2 tablespoons	2 tablespoons

Peel cucumber and slice very thinly. Place in a bowl, sprinkle with salt and stand for at least 30 minutes. Press out all the liquid and if too salty, rinse with cold water. Drain well. Mix with remaining ingredients and serve as an accompaniment to a curry meal.

brinjal pahi

Eggplant Pickle

Ingredients	Metric	Imperial
Eggplants	2 large	2 large
Salt	2 teaspoons	2 teaspoons
Ground turmeric	2 teaspoons	2 teaspoons
Oil	for frying	for frying
Black mustard seed	1 tablespoon	1 tablespoon
Vinegar	100 ml	½ cup
Onion, finely chopped	1 medium	1 medium
Garlic, sliced	4 cloves	4 cloves
Finely chopped fresh root ginger	1 tablespoon	1 tablespoon
Ground coriander	1 tablespoon	1 tablespoon
Ground cummin	2 teaspoons	2 teaspoons
Ground fennel	1 teaspoon	1 teaspoon
Tamarind pulp	100 ml	½ cup
Hot water	150 ml	¾ cup
Fresh chillies, seeded and sliced	3	3
Cinnamon stick	8 cm piece	3-inch piece
Chilli powder (optional)	1 teaspoon	1 teaspoon
Sugar	2 teaspoons	2 teaspoons
Extra salt	to taste	to taste

Cut eggplants into thin slices, rub with salt and turmeric and place in a bowl. Stand for 1 hour at least. Pour off liquid that collects and drain eggplant on paper towels. Heat approximately 2.5 cm (1-inch) oil in a frying pan and fry the slices of eggplant quite slowly until brown on both sides. Lift out with a slotted spoon and place in a dry bowl. Reserve oil used for frying.

Place mustard seed and vinegar in blender container, cover and blend on high speed until mustard is ground. Add onion, garlic and ginger, cover and blend again until a smooth paste is formed. Set aside.

Place coriander, cummin and fennel in a small dry pan and heat gently, shaking pan or stirring frequently, until medium brown in colour. (If preferred, substitute 1½ tablespoons Ceylon curry powder for these ingredients.)

Squeeze tamarind pulp in hot water, strain and discard seeds, reserve liquid.

Heat ½ cup of reserved oil and fry the blended mixture for 5 minutes. Add coriander mixture or curry powder, chillies, cinnamon stick, chilli powder if used and tamarind liquid. Add fried eggplant slices and any oil that has collected in the bowl, stir well, cover and simmer for 15 minutes. Remove from heat, stir in sugar. Add extra salt to taste if necessary.

Cool thoroughly and store in clean, dry jars.

fried eggplant sambol

Prepare eggplant slices as for Brinjal Pahi (see page 46). Fry in hot oil and drain on absorbent paper. Mix with seeded and chopped chillies, finely sliced onion, lemon juice to taste and 3 tablespoons thick Coconut Milk (see page 66).

prawn blachan

This is an essential accompaniment to Lampries, (see page 35), the festive meal wrapped in banana leaves.

Serves: 18-20

Ingredients	Metric	Imperial
Dried prawn powder	200 ml	1 cup
Desiccated coconut	100 ml	½ cup
Chilli powder	2 teaspoons or to taste	2 teaspoons or to taste
Onions, chopped	2 medium	2 medium
Garlic, sliced	5 cloves	5 cloves
Finely chopped fresh root ginger	1 tablespoon	1 tablespoon
Lemon juice	134 ml	⅔ cup
Salt	1 teaspoon or to taste	1 teaspoon or to taste

Place prawn powder in a dry frying pan and heat for a few minutes, stirring continuously. Turn on to a large plate. Place desiccated coconut in the same pan and heat, stirring constantly, until a rich brown colour. Turn out on to plate to cool. Place remaining ingredients into blender container, cover and blend until smooth. Add prawn powder and desiccated coconut, cover and blend again, adding a little water if necessary to bind ingredients together. Scrape down sides of container with a spatula from time to time. Turn on to a plate and form into a round, flat cake. Serve with rice and curries.

vattalappam

Spicy Coconut Custard.

This rich custard, Malayan in origin, is very popular in Ceylon. If jaggery (also known as palm sugar or goela djawa) is not available, substitute with 100 ml (½ cup) firmly packed black sugar and 100 ml (½ cup) maple syrup.

Serves: 6-8
Cooking time: approximately 1¼ hours.
Oven temperature: 150-160°C (300-325°F)

Ingredients	Metric	Imperial
Eggs	4	4
Jaggery	125 g	5 oz
Water	100 ml	½ cup
Thick Coconut Milk (see below)	300 ml	1½ cups
Evaporated milk	150 ml	¾ cup
Ground cardamom	½ teaspoon	½ teaspoon
Ground mace	¼ teaspoon	¼ teaspoon
Ground cloves	pinch	pinch
Rose water	1 tablespoon	1 tablespoon

Beat eggs slightly, (they should not be frothy). Dissolve jaggery in water over a low heat, cool slightly. Add jaggery syrup or black sugar and maple syrup to beaten eggs, add the coconut milk and stir to dissolve sugar.

Strain through a fine strainer into a large jug, add evaporated milk, spices and rose water. Pour into individual custard cups.

Place custard cups in a baking dish with water to come half-way up sides of cups and bake in a slow oven to set, approximately 1¼ hours.

Alternatively, put the same depth of water into an electric frypan. Set temperature to 120°C (260°F), place custard cups in, cover and cook until set, approximately 1¼ hours.
Cool and chill custards before serving.

<u>Coconut Milk:</u> For this custard, the coconut milk is made with milk instead of water. Place 400 ml (2 cups) desiccated coconut in a saucepan, pour over 500 ml (2½ cups) milk and bring slowly to the boil. Cool to lukewarm, then extract Coconut Milk (see page 66). Only use the first extract in this recipe.

potato halva

This is an ideal sweetmeat to eat after a rich curry meal. Serve with black coffee.

Ingredients	Metric	Imperial
Sugar	300 ml	1½ cups
Milk	300 ml	1½ cups
Sweetened condensed milk	1 x 410 g can	1 x 14½ oz can
Ghee or butter	100 g	4 oz
Prepared instant mashed potato	200 ml	1 cup
Finely chopped cashew nuts (optional)	200 ml	1 cup
Rose water	2 tablespoons	2 tablespoons
Ground cardamom	1 teaspoon	1 teaspoon

Place sugar, milk, condensed milk and ghee into a large heavy saucepan (a non-stick pan is excellent for this). Cook, stirring continuously, until mixture reaches soft ball stage or 116°C (240°F) on a candy thermometer. Remove from heat, add potato and nuts if used. Return to heat and cook until mixture reaches soft ball stage or 116°C (240°F) again. Remove from heat, add rose water and cardamom and mix well.

Pour into a greased shallow dish. Press lightly with a piece of greased aluminium foil to smooth and flatten the surface. Allow to set, then cut into diamond shapes.

burma

A Burmese meal is most often plain white rice served with curries and balachaung—crisply fried dried prawns. Or boiled noodles swimming in a fragrant soup over which is sprinkled a choice of accompaniments.

Curry powders are unknown in Burmese cookery and curries are based on onions, garlic, ginger and chillies combined in varying proportions. Unlike the curries of India, Burmese curries are rather liquid and are generally more delicately flavoured.

I was too young to remember my first visit to my grandmother's home in Rangoon, Burma, but the second visit which lasted a year has left a medley of impressions. I remember the two-storey house set back in its garden and kept cool by ceiling fans and wooden Venetians at the windows; the staircase of polished dark wood which seemed so high I never dared slide down the balustrade; the spacious rooms so typical of homes in the tropics, and the quiet orderliness of life under my grandmother's stern but loving reign.

My most vivid memories of Burma are of food. I recall saving my pocket money to buy snacks from the unending stream of vendors who walked the suburban streets calling their wares. There was pau-see—a steamed bun with sweet black bean filling, my favourite; ice-lollies made to order with shaved ice and brightly coloured syrup; kulfi ice cream rich with clotted cream and flavoured with rose essence, unmoulded from cone-shaped metal containers packed in ice.

In the evenings we often walked in the bazaar area where the streets were lined with food stalls of every kind. Snacks, sweets, cool drinks, complete meals—each stall specialized in one particular item. What I liked best was fresh sugar cane juice extracted between large, shiny steel rollers as you watched and poured onto crushed ice clinking in tall glasses.

At home, our meals followed a certain pattern. Breakfast was most often rice boiled in coconut milk followed by fresh fruit—bananas, mangoes, mangosteens or other fruit in season.

Lunch was a simple meal of rice and curry. Dinner, served around 8 o'clock, was sometimes western style (we had an Indian cook whose repertoire was quite extensive) and sometimes one of the Burmese specialities like Kowshwe, Mohinga or Chah-Zan.

Garlic is used liberally in Burmese food and all cooking is done in sesame oil, but it is a much lighter sesame oil than is generally available here and I suggest using peanut oil with a small amount of sesame oil to flavour it.

The recipes that follow, for which I am indebted to my mother, will enable you to capture the true flavour of Burmese food.

panthé kowshwé

A popular Burmese dish that particularly appeals to Westerners. Panthe Kowshwé is a mild curry with lots of gravy. It is ladled over a bowl of egg noodles and served with a number of accompaniments with contrasting flavours.

Serves: 6-8

Ingredients	Metric	Imperial
Chicken or chicken pieces	1.2 kg	3 lb
Garlic, chopped	5 cloves	5 cloves
Onions, chopped	3 medium	3 medium
Finely chopped fresh root ginger	1 tablespoon	1 tablespoon
Ngapi or blachan	1 teaspoon	1 teaspoon
Peanut oil	2 tablespoons	2 tablespoons
Sesame oil	1 tablespoon	1 tablespoon
Chilli powder	1-2 teaspoons	1-2 teaspoons
Salt	2 teaspoons	2 teaspoons
Thin Coconut Milk (see page 66)	400 ml	2 cups
Thick Coconut Milk (see page 66)	400 ml	2 cups
Besan (lentil flour)	2 tablespoons	2 tablespoons
Thin egg noodles	400 g	1 lb
Accompaniments (see page 54)		

Cut chicken into serving pieces. Place garlic, onion, ginger and ngapi into blender container, cover and blend until smooth, adding 1 tablespoon of the peanut oil if necessary. Heat remaining oil and fry the blended ingredients for 5 minutes. Add chicken and continue to fry, stirring constantly. Add chilli powder, salt and thin coconut milk. Cover and simmer until chicken is tender, adding a little hot water if mixture becomes dry. Add thick coconut milk, return to the heat and bring slowly to the boil, stirring continuously to prevent the mixture from curdling. Mix besan with a little cold water to a smooth cream, add to the curry and cook for a further 5 minutes, uncovered. (There should be a lot of gravy.)
Just before serving, cook noodles in a large saucepan of boiling salted water until just tender, approximately 5-6 minutes. Pour cold water into pan to stop noodles cooking, drain in a colander.

Serve noodles in a large bowl and the curry in a separate bowl. Serve accompaniments in small bowls. Each person takes a serving of noodles, ladles on a generous amount of the curry and sprinkles various accompaniments over the top.

mohinga

The national dish of Burma, Mohinga is to the Burmese what onion soup is to the French. Bowls of Mohinga are a popular snack sold at roadside stalls or by vendors who carry their cooking apparatus from house to house.

It can be made with canned bamboo shoots, but in Burma it is made with the tender heart of a banana tree (an ingredient rather hard to come by in Australia).

My grandmother, who was born in Burma and lived most of her life there, would not let a little thing like that deter her. When she came to Australia she was in her seventies. One day she decided Mohinga would be on the menu, went into the garden and cut down a banana tree herself. For such a feminine person, she was very self-reliant. The feast she prepared brought back memories of the land of golden pagodas.

If you are determined to make this dish in the true Burmese fashion, use the top portion of the banana tree, just under the leaves. Protect your hands with gloves and put on your oldest clothes, because it leaves a nasty stain. Peel off the outer layers and use about 30 cm (12-inches) of the tender heart of the tree. Cut in half lengthways, then in thin crossways strips. Soak in salted water for several hours.

Serves: 8

Ingredients	Metric	Imperial
Peanut oil	4 tablespoons	4 tablespoons
Sesame oil	2 tablespoons	2 tablespoons
Onions, sliced	4 medium	4 medium
Garlic, chopped	4 cloves	4 cloves
Fresh chillies, seeded and chopped	2	2
Ngapi or blachan	1 teaspoon	1 teaspoon
Thin Coconut Milk (see page 66)	800 ml	4 cups
Fresh fish fillets or	4	4
herrings in tomato sauce	1 x 200 g can	1 x 7 oz can
Salt	2 teaspoons	2 teaspoons
Bamboo shoots	1 x 255 g can	1 x 9 oz can
Besan (lentil flour)	3 tablespoons	3 tablespoons
Thick Coconut Milk (see page 66)	400 ml	2 cups
Lemon juice	2 tablespoons	2 tablespoons
Extra salt	to taste	to taste
Egg noodles	400 g	1 lb
Accompaniments (see page 54)		

Heat peanut and sesame oil and fry onion and garlic until soft. Add chillies and ngapi and fry 2 minutes longer. Add thin coconut milk, fish and salt. (If using canned fish, add liquid from can as well.) Drain bamboo shoots, cut in half lengthways and across into very thin slices, add to mixture. Bring to the boil, lower heat and simmer 15 minutes. Stir in besan mixed to a smooth cream with a little cold water, simmer 5 minutes longer. Add thick coconut milk and lemon juice. Season to taste with extra salt if necessary.

Cook noodles in boiling salted water until just tender, drain well. Serve in a bowl.

Serve fish soup in a separate bowl or tureen. Provide deep bowls for eating from, rather than plates. Noodles are served first and soup ladled over the top. Mohinga must be served piping hot. Pass accompaniments separately so guests can make their own choice.

hin-chyo

Vegetable Soup

This is a very delicately flavoured soup, not served as a first course, but alongside rice and curry and added a spoonful at a time, as desired.

Serves: 8

Ingredients	Metric	Imperial
Water	1 litre	5 cups
Prawn powder or	1 tablespoon	1 tablespoon
large prawns	6	6
Onions sliced	2 medium	2 medium
Ngapi	½ teaspoon	½ teaspoon
Salt	to taste	to taste
Marrow, cucumber or zucchini, thinly sliced	400 g	1 lb

Place water, prawn powder, onion and ngapi into a saucepan and bring to the boil. Cook until onion is soft. Add salt to taste. Add marrow and cook until tender.

chah-zan

The main ingredient in this dish is cellophane noodles. Fine, transparent and with no flavour of their own, the flavour accent is on what you eat with them. They are served with Panthé Kowshwé curry or Mohinga soup and appropriate accompaniments.

Serves: 6-8

Ingredients	Metric	Imperial
Cellophane noodles	300 g	12 oz
Panthé Kowshwé curry (see page 51) or		
Mohinga soup (see page 52)		
Accompaniments (see below)		
Lemon wedges		

Prepare Panthé Kowshwé curry or Mohinga soup.

Bring a large saucepan of salted water to the boil, drop in the noodles and cook for 20 minutes. Drain. Serve in a large bowl. (Serving is easier if the noodles are cut into shorter lengths with a sharp knife.)

Each person places some noodles in a bowl, ladles Panthé Kowshwé curry or Mohinga soup over and adds whichever accompaniments he pleases. Everything is mixed together and a lemon wedge squeezed over to add piquancy. The crisp fried chillies are held by the stalk and bitten into (with caution please, if this is your first experience) when a hot mouthful is desired.

Accompaniments to Chah-Zan, Panthé Kowshwé, Mohinga and Kowshwé:

Finely sliced shallots, both green and white portion.
Chopped fresh coriander leaves.
Finely sliced white onions.
Roasted chick peas, finely ground in a blender, or crushed with a mortar and pestle.
Crisp fried noodles, broken into small pieces.
Fried onion flakes.
Thin slices of garlic, fried in oil until golden.
Lemon wedges.
Dried chillies, fried in oil for 3-4 seconds.
Chilli powder.

Note: Roasted chick peas are sold in Greek delicatessen shops.

prawn and bamboo shoot curry

Serves: 6

Ingredients	Metric	Imperial
Raw prawns	600 g	1½ lb
Bamboo shoots	1 x 255 g can	1 x 9 oz can
Gravy:		
Sesame oil	50 g	¼ cup
Onions, finely chopped	3 medium	3 medium
Garlic, finely chopped	6 cloves	6 cloves
Finely chopped fresh root ginger	1 tablespoon	1 tablespoon
Ground turmeric	1 teaspoon	1 teaspoon
Chilli powder (optional)	1-2 teaspoons	1-2 teaspoons
Paprika pepper (optional)	1 teaspoon	1 teaspoon
Tomatoes, peeled and chopped	2	2
Salt	1½ teaspoons	1½ teaspoons
Ngapi or blachan	1 teaspoon	1 teaspoon
Hot water	300 ml	1½ cups
Chopped fresh coriander	2 tablespoons	2 tablespoons
Lemon juice	2 tablespoons	2 tablespoons

Shell and de-vein prawns. Drain bamboo shoots and cut into thin strips or small dice.

Gravy: Heat oil and fry onion, garlic and ginger until soft and beginning to turn golden. Add turmeric, remove from heat and add chilli powder and paprika pepper if used, tomato and salt. (In Burmese cooking, the amount of chilli powder used would be enough to give a red colour to the curry, but the paprika pepper is suggested here as a substitute for a portion of it, with chilli powder used to suit individual taste.)

Wrap ngapi in aluminium foil and cook under a hot grill for a few minutes on each side. Unwrap, dissolve in the hot water and add to the curry. Cook until tomato is soft and pulpy.

Add prawns and bamboo shoots, cook for a further 20 minutes. Sprinkle with chopped coriander and lemon juice, mix thoroughly and cook 5 minutes longer. Serve with boiled white rice and accompaniments.

fish kofta curry

My grandmother taught me how to make this most delicious of all fish curries. There is no use pretending it is a quick and easy recipe, but it is the tastiest way of serving fish. For a more delicate dish, poach the fish koftas in simmering water and serve as a fish soup accompanied by boiled rice.

Serves: 6

Ingredients	Metric	Imperial
Fish Koftas:		
Jewfish or cod fillets	400 g	2 lb
Salt	2½ teaspoons	2½ teaspoons
Pepper	½ teaspoon	½ teaspoon
Onion, finely chopped	1 medium	1 medium
Garlic, crushed	1 large clove	1 large clove
Finely grated fresh root ginger	1½ teaspoons	1½ teaspoons
Lemon juice, strained	2 tablespoons	2 tablespoons
Finely chopped fresh coriander or dill	1 tablespoon	1 tablespoon
White bread soaked in hot water and squeezed dry	2 slices	2 slices
Anchovy paste or sauce (optional)	1 teaspoon	1 teaspoon
Monosodium glutamate	½ teaspoon	½ teaspoon
Gravy (see Prawn and Bamboo Shoot Curry, page 55)		

Fish Koftas: With a sharp knife or Chinese chopper, remove skin from fish. Finely mince fish fillets, taking care to remove any bones. (The easiest way to do this without a mincer, is to cut the fillets in thin slices lengthways, then chop finely across.) Place in a large bowl, add remaining ingredients and mix thoroughly with the hands. Shape the mixture into walnut-size balls or koftas. (This quantity will make 24 koftas.)

Gravy: (See Prawn and Bamboo Shoot Curry, page 55). Proceed until tomato is soft and pulpy. If gravy seems too reduced, add a little hot water. There should be enough gravy to almost cover the fish koftas. Gently place the fish koftas in the gravy and simmer over a moderate heat until they are cooked, approximately 20 minutes. Shake pan gently from time to time. Do not stir until fish is cooked and firm as the koftas may break. Serve with boiled rice and Balachaung (see page 58).

nam prik

making coconut milk

gin letho

The Burmese, a very relaxed race, sit around talking for a long time after each meal. Instead of a sweet dessert, they partake of digestive 'nibbles like Gin Letho. I have served it at dinner parties and found it enthusiastically received by my guests.

Ingredients	Metric	Imperial
Fresh young root ginger	100 g	4 oz
Lemon juice	4 tablespoons	4 tablespoons
Peanut oil	2 tablespoons	2 tablespoons
Sesame oil	1 tablespoon	1 tablespoon
Garlic, sliced	12 cloves	12 cloves
Sesame seeds	2-3 tablespoons	2-3 tablespoons
Salt	to taste	to taste

Ideally, the ginger root should be very young and tender—at the stage when the skin is almost transparent and the roots are tipped with pink. If the ginger you buy is more mature, use the small knobs growing off the main root. (The rest of the ginger may be peeled and preserved in a jar by covering with dry sherry.) Scrape skin off ginger with a sharp knife and cut into very thin slices. Cut the slices into fine slivers and marinate in lemon juice for at least 1 hour.

Meanwhile, heat peanut and sesame oil in a small frying pan and fry the sliced garlic slowly until pale golden. Remove from heat immediately (they burn easily) and drain on absorbent paper. Allow to cool and become crisp. Place the sesame seeds in a dry frying pan and stir continuously over a moderate heat until golden brown. Turn immediately on to a plate to cool.

When ready to serve, drain ginger from lemon juice and place in a bowl. Add salt to taste and sprinkle with garlic and sesame seeds. Toss together lightly. Each person takes a pinch of the combined ingredients and nibbles. It is supposedly very good for the digestion.

kowshwé

Fried noodles with meat and vegetables—a one dish meal.

Serves: 6-8

Ingredients	Metric	Imperial
Lard or bacon fat	200 ml	1 cup
Onions, sliced	4 medium	4 medium
Cabbage, shredded	½ medium	½ medium
Chicken, cut into joints	1 x 1.2 kg	1 x 3 lb
Pork, cut into fine strips	200 g	8 oz
Salt	2 teaspoons or to taste	2 teaspoons or to taste
Water	200 ml	1 cup
Chilli powder (optional)	1 teaspoon	1 teaspoon
Egg noodles	400 g	1 lb
Accompaniments (see page 54)		

Heat lard in a large saucepan and fry the onion and cabbage until soft. Add chicken and pork and fry, stirring continuously, for 10 minutes. Add salt, water and chilli powder if used. Cover and cook over a low heat for 35-40 minutes or until chicken is tender. Uncover pan and cook until liquid evaporates and oil separates from mixture. Lift out chicken pieces.

Cook noodles in boiling salted water until just tender, pour some cold water into pan to stop noodles cooking and drain thoroughly in a colander. Add noodles to pan containing cabbage and pork mixture and toss to combine ingredients thoroughly.

Arrange chicken pieces on top and serve hot. Pass accompanments separately.

balachaung

A very crisp fried prawn preparation served as an accompaniment to rice.

Ingredients	Metric	Imperial
Garlic	20 cloves	20 cloves
Onions, finely sliced	2 medium	2 medium
Peanut oil	400 ml	2 cups
Prawn powder	1 x 225 g packet	1 x 8 oz packet
Chilli powder (optional)	2 teaspoons	2 teaspoons
Salt	2 teaspoons or to taste	2 teaspoons or to taste
Vinegar	100 ml	½ cup

Peel garlic, cut into thin slices. Cut onions into thin, even-size slices. Heat oil and fry onion and garlic separately until golden brown. Lift out immediately and set aside. They will become crisp as they cool.

In the same oil, fry the prawn powder for 5 minutes. Add chilli powder and salt mixed with the vinegar, stir well and fry until prawn mixture is crisp. Allow to cool completely. Mix in the fried onion and garlic, stirring to distribute evenly. Balachaung may be kept for months in an air-tight jar.

molosaung

A cooling drink of sago, coconut milk and goela djawa (palm sugar) which may be served as a dessert.

Ingredients	Metric	Imperial
Sago	200 ml	1 cup
Water	800 ml	4 cups
Goela djawa	1 x 140 g packet	1 x 5 oz packet
Ice cubes		
Coconut Milk (see page 66)	800 ml	4 cups

Wash and soak sago for approximately 1 hour, drain and place in a large saucepan with 600 ml (3 cups) of the water. Bring to the boil and simmer over a moderate heat until sago grains are clear. Cool and chill.

Place goela djawa in a small saucepan with remaining water and heat gently until cakes of sugar dissolve. Cool the syrup.

For each serving, place approximately 4 tablespoons chilled sago into a tall glass, add 3 tablespoons syrup (or more according to taste) and mix well. Add 2-3 cubes of ice and fill up with coconut milk. Stir and serve immediately.

thailand

As in other South East Asian countries, the mainstay of a Thai meal is rice or noodles. Vegetables, pork, seafood, poultry and a variety of sweet-sour or hot sauces are served with the rice.

There are two ingredients always present in Thai food as in Burmese food—prawn paste and coriander herb. Each is pungent, and the uninitiated cook may be tempted to omit them. Resist the temptation. When added to food in correct quantities, they give the individuality which characterizes the food of mainland South East Asia.

I remember, as a school girl in Ceylon and Burma, that when I visited the tuckshop it was not to buy cakes and sweets. Rather, we used to munch unripe mangoes or sour olives, dipped in a mixture of salt and chilli powder. In Thailand too, their nibbles are hot, salty, sour. They dip green mango slices in a fish sauce as the Burmese do with their nampi-yah-yay. It may be an acquired taste, but it is only too easy to become addicted.

A typical Thai meal will be based on White Rice (see page 67). This is served with a curry similar to a Burmese curry; a fried noodle dish such as Mi Krob (see page 63); a soup (see page 62 or page 53); and a sharp-flavoured accompaniment such as Nam Prik sauce (see page 64) with raw or boiled vegetables, or a salad of sliced green mangoes or other acid fruit (try tart apples) mixed with cooked diced pork or prawns and flavoured with nam-pla (a fish sauce), tamarind juice and chilli powder.

garlic chicken

This may sound like a lot of garlic and pepper, but the result is so unusual and delicious that I hesitate to modify the recipe. The coarsely crushed peppercorns are not as hot as the same amount of finely ground pepper.

Serves: 4-5

Ingredients	Metric	Imperial
Roasting chicken or	1 x 1.6 kg	1 x 4 lb
chicken breasts	800 g	2 lb
Garlic	6 cloves	6 cloves
Salt	2 teaspoons	2 teaspoons
Peppercorns	1 tablespoon	1 tablespoon
Whole plants fresh coriander herb	4	4
Lemon juice	2 tablespoons	2 tablespoons

Cut chicken into serving pieces, or cut breasts in halves. Crush garlic with the salt. Coarsely crush peppercorns with a mortar and pestle or in a blender. Finely chop the well washed coriander—roots, stems and leaves. Mix all the seasonings together and rub well into the chicken pieces. Cover and stand for 1 hour at least, or refrigerate overnight.
Place pieces of chicken on a grill tray and place under a hot grill, approximately 15 cm (6-inches) from heat. Cook, turning every 5 minutes, until chicken is tender and skin is crisp. (If possible, cook on a barbecue over glowing coals.)

Serve with boiled rice, fresh tomato sambal (sliced or diced tomato seasoned with a pinch of chilli powder, salt and lemon juice) or thinly sliced onion.

kung tom yam

Prawn Soup

Serves: 4

Ingredients	Metric	Imperial
Raw prawns	800 g	2 lb
Oil	1 tablespoon	1 tablespoon
Hot water	1.2 litres	6 cups
Salt	1 teaspoon	1 teaspoon
Dried lemon grass	12 strips	12 strips
Ngapi or blachan	½ teaspoon	½ teaspoon
Sambal oelek	1 teaspoon	1 teaspoon
Fresh chilli, seeded and sliced	1	1
Chopped fresh coriander	2 tablespoons	2 tablespoons

Shell and de-vein prawns. Wash prawn heads well, drain. Heat oil in saucepan and fry heads and shells of prawns until they turn pink, add hot water and salt and bring to the boil. Cover and simmer for 20 minutes. Strain and reserve stock, discard heads and shells.

Add all remaining ingredients except coriander to stock and simmer for 10 minutes or until prawns are cooked. Remove lemon grass just before serving and sprinkle with chopped coriander.

mí krob

Crisp Fried Vermicelli

Serves: 6-8

Ingredients	Metric	Imperial
Oil	for deep frying	for deep frying
Rice vermicelli	200 g	8 oz
Chinese mushrooms	12	12
Dried wood fungus	100 ml	½ cup
Lean pork	200 g	8 oz
Whole chicken breast	1	1
Raw prawns	200 g	8 oz
Shallots	12	12
Green beans	12	12
Extra oil	3 tablespoons	3 tablespoons
Garlic, finely chopped	3 cloves	3 cloves
Onion, finely chopped	1 medium	1 medium
Soy sauce	4 tablespoons	4 tablespoons
Sugar	1 tablespoon	1 tablespoon
Vinegar	4 tablespoons	4 tablespoons
Ngapi or anchovy sauce	1 teaspoon 2 tablespoons	1 teaspoon 2 tablespoons
Sambal oelek	1 teaspoon	1 teaspoon
Chopped fresh coriander	4 tablespoons	4 tablespoons

Heat oil in a wok. Break vermicelli into pieces and deep fry in oil. The oil should be very hot so vermicelli puffs and swells immediately. (If this does not happen it will be tough and difficult to eat, so test heat of oil with a little vermicelli first.) Turn vermicelli and fry other side. Lift out and drain on absorbent paper.

Soak dried mushrooms and fungus separately in hot water for 20 minutes, remove and discard stems of mushrooms and slice. Drain fungus well, squeezing out excess water.

Finely shred pork. Bone and shred chicken breast. Shell and de-vein prawns and cut into large pieces. Cut shallots (green part included) into 2.5 cm (1-inch) pieces. String beans and cut in very thin diagonal slices.

Heat extra oil in wok, fry garlic and onion for 3 minutes and when they begin to colour, add pork and fry for 8-10 minutes, stirring continuously. Add chicken and prawns. Continue to fry, stirring continuously, until they change colour and are cooked. Add shallots and beans, fry for 1 minute. Mix soy sauce, sugar, vinegar, ngapi and sambal oelek together. Add to pan and stir for 2 minutes. Add vermicelli, toss all ingredients together and serve immediately, sprinkled with chopped coriander.

Note: Ngapi and soy sauce may be omitted and 3 tablespoons nam-pla (fish sauce) used instead.

nam prik

Thai Shrimp Sauce

Favourite sauce of a sauce-loving people, Nam Prik is what the Thais use to season almost everything they eat. It is pungent and perhaps strange to the western palate. Try it as a dip for a first course of attractively arranged boiled prawns, green beans cooked until just tender, fried fish pieces, raw sliced vegetables such as radish and cucumber, spring onions served with part of the green leaves, and wedges of hard-boiled egg. For each person, provide a small bowl of boiled rice which is eaten between mouthfuls.

Ingredients	Metric	Imperial
Dried shrimps	2 tablespoons	2 tablespoons
Ngapi or blachan	1 teaspoon	1 teaspoon
Garlic	4 cloves	4 cloves
Fresh chillies, seeded or sambal oelek	1-2	1-2
	2 teaspoons	2 teaspoons
Black sugar	2 teaspoons	2 teaspoons
Lemon juice	2 tablespoons	2 tablespoons
Soy sauce	1½ tablespoons	1½ tablespoons
Water	3 tablespoons	3 tablespoons

Wash shrimps and soak in hot water for 20 minutes. De-vein and rinse the shrimps thoroughly. Press ngapi into a flat cake, wrap in aluminium foil and place under a hot grill for approximately 3 minutes on each side. Place drained shrimps and grilled ngapi in blender container with garlic, chillies, sugar, lemon juice, soy sauce and water. Cover and blend until smooth. Pour into a bowl and serve with other ingredients arranged around.

If blender is not available, pound the shrimps, crush the garlic and use sambal oelek instead of fresh chillies. After grilling, dissolve ngapi in the soy sauce and then combine all the ingredients thoroughly.

indonesia

This exotic string of islands—some supporting more than 60 million people and others mere specks in the ocean—has much to offer the adventurous eater in the way of new flavours, textures and food combinations. Because its people are widely separated due to geographical factors, different influences have shaped the food of the islands and Indonesian food is infinitely varied. Some dishes are very hot, others mild but—as befits food that originated in the Spice Islands, as the Indonesian archipelago was called by Marco Polo—they are always fragrant with spices and other flavourings.

An Indonesian meal always features rice. Whatever else is served, rice is always the foundation of the meal. Learn to cook it the Oriental way, that is, by the absorption method (see page 67). It has so much more flavour than rice that is cooked in water and drained. It also has an appealing chewy texture and pearly appearance.

With the rice it is customary to serve a fish or meat curry (or both), two or more vegetable dishes, krupuk or prawn crisps (bought in packets and deep fried in hot oil) and sambals.

Many popular Indonesian sambals are available in Australian stores and since the making of these involves the handling of large quantities of fresh chillies (this can be a searing experience if one is the slightest bit careless), I would recommend that you buy these sambals in bottles. They are not expensive and are eaten in such minute quantities that it is hardly worth the trouble to make them. When you handle hot chillies in these recipes, even one or two, please equip yourself with disposable gloves. If you do forget and touch the chillies, keep your hands away from your eyes, your skin and especially your baby.

Thanks to the interest in all things Indonesian, it is fairly easy to obtain the ingredients mentioned in these recipes. You should have to look no further than a large store with a gourmet food department, a Chinese grocery store or a go-ahead delicatessen.

coconut milk

Coconut Milk is such an important ingredient in Indonesian cookery that I will explain the various methods of extracting it.

I have heard so many people refer to the clear liquid inside a coconut as the milk that, at the risk of boring those in the know, I'll tell you what Coconut Milk really is. It's the milky liquid extracted from the grated flesh of fresh coconuts or reconstituted from desiccated coconut.

Before I start to cook, I make all the Coconut Milk I am going to need and strongly advise this routine. (It gets this job out of the way when you are fresh and enthusiastic and doesn't stop you in your tracks in the middle of a recipe.)

Using Desiccated Coconut: A lot of cooks use desiccated coconut. Nine times out of ten I do too. It is much easier and quicker to prepare than grating fresh coconut and in curries you cannot tell the difference.

To make Coconut Milk from desiccated coconut, place 400 ml (2 cups) desiccated coconut in a bowl and pour over 500 ml (2½ cups) hot water. Allow to cool until lukewarm, then knead firmly with the hand for a few minutes and strain through a fine strainer or piece of muslin, squeezing out as much liquid as possible. This should produce approximately 300 ml (1½ cups) thick Coconut Milk.

Repeat the process, using the same coconut and 500 ml (2½ cups) more hot water. This second extract will produce approximately 400 ml (2 cups) thin Coconut Milk. (Because of the moisture retained in the coconut the first time, the second extraction usually yields more milk.)

Using a Blender: With an electric blender you save time and a lot of hard kneading. Place 400 ml (2 cups) desiccated coconut and 500 ml (2½ cups) hot water in blender container, cover and blend for 30 seconds. Strain through a fine strainer or piece of muslin. Repeat process, using the same coconut and 500 ml (2½ cups) more hot water.

Note: If a richer milk is required, as in coconut desserts such as Vattalappam (see page 48), milk replaces the water and only the first extract is used. The second extract may be used in other dishes.

Using Fresh Coconut: In Asian countries, fresh coconut is used. Grating fresh coconut is easy if you have the right implement for the job. There are various types of coconut graters and the most successful one, and easiest to use, screws on to the edge of a table, like a mincing machine. It has a number of curving, serrated blades which meet at a central point like a citrus juice extractor. By turning the handle with one hand and holding a half coconut in position with the other, it is possible to grate all the white flesh with no danger of slipping knives or skinned knuckles.

To extract the Coconut Milk, pour a little hot water over the grated coconut and knead thoroughly. Add more hot water as required. Strain. Repeat process a second and a third time, using the same coconut and more hot water. The second and third extracts, known as thin milk, are also used for cooking and impart a good flavour though not as much richness as the first extract.

Note: When Coconut Milk is called for in recipes, use a mixture of first and second extracts unless 'Thick' milk or 'Thin' milk is specified.

ground coconut

Coconut is also used for adding thickness and flavour to curry gravies. In most recipes, it is toasted first until golden brown.

Place desiccated coconut in a dry frying pan and stir constantly over a moderate heat until the coconut is a rich golden brown. Spread immediately on a plate to cool.

If an electric blender is available, grind the coconut with a little liquid on high speed before adding to curry. Approximately 2 tablespoons is used in an average curry.

nasi

White Rice

Serves: 6-8

Ingredients	Metric	Imperial
Short grain rice	400 ml	2 cups
Water	400 ml	2 cups
Salt	2 teaspoons	2 teaspoons

Wash rice in plenty of cold water, change water 4-5 times. Pour rice into a strainer and allow to drain well.

Put water and salt into a saucepan with a well-fitting lid and bring to the boil. Add rice, return to the boil, then stir once or twice. Turn heat very low, cover saucepan tightly and cook for 20 minutes. Do not lift lid while cooking.

nasi goreng

Fried Rice

Serves: 6-8

Ingredients	Metric	Imperial
Eggs	3	3
Salt and pepper	to taste	to taste
Oil	for frying	for frying
Onions	2 medium	2 medium
Garlic	2 cloves	2 cloves
Trasi or blachan	½ teaspoon	½ teaspoon
Extra oil	5 tablespoons	5 tablespoons
Raw prawns	200 g	8 oz
Lean steak or pork	400 g	1 lb
Shallots, chopped	6	6
Cold boiled rice	800 ml	4 cups
Soy sauce	2 tablespoons	2 tablespoons
Dried onion flakes, fried until golden brown in oil	3 tablespoons	3 tablespoons
Green cucumber, thinly sliced	1	1

Beat eggs with salt and pepper to taste. Heat a little oil in a frying pan and make an omelet with half the beaten eggs. Turn on to a plate to cool (do not fold omelet). Repeat process with remaining beaten eggs. When cool, place one omelet on top of the other, roll up and cut into thin strips.

Chop onions roughly and place in blender container with garlic and trasi. Cover and blend to a paste. (If blender is not available, finely chop onions and garlic and dissolve trasi in a little hot water. Combine these ingredients.)

Heat 3 tablespoons of the extra oil in a large frying pan or wok and fry the blended ingredients until cooked. Shell and de-vein prawns, cut steak or pork into fine strips. Add prawns and meat to pan and fry, stirring continuously, until they are cooked. Add remaining 2 tablespoons of extra oil, and when hot, stir in the shallots and rice, mixing thoroughly and frying until it is very hot. Sprinkle with soy sauce and mix evenly.

Serve the fried rice garnished with strips of omelet, fried onion flakes and very thin slices of cucumber.

Note: Fry dried onion flakes for a few seconds only. Remove from heat at once as they burn easily.

ikan bandeng

Baked Fish

If you can beg or borrow some large banana leaves to wrap the fish in, do so. They give a subtle and appetizing fragrance and look exotic when the dish is served at the table.

Serves: 4
Cooking time: 35-40 minutes
Oven temperature: 170-190°C (350-375°F)

Ingredients	Metric	Imperial
Spanish mackerel, snapper or jewfish	1 medium	1 medium
Onion, chopped	1 medium	1 medium
Garlic	2 cloves	2 cloves
Finely chopped fresh root ginger	1 teaspoon	1 teaspoon
Tamarind liquid	2 tablespoons	2 tablespoons
Soy sauce	1 tablespoon	1 tablespoon
Oil	1 tablespoon	1 tablespoon
Sambal oelek (optional)	1 teaspoon	1 teaspoon
Salt	1 teaspoon	1 teaspoon
Ground turmeric	1 teaspoon	1 teaspoon
Finely chopped fresh coriander	3 tablespoons	3 tablespoons

Wash fish and dry well with paper towels. Score the flesh diagonally on each side.

Place onion, garlic, ginger, tamarind liquid, soy sauce, oil, sambal oelek if used, salt and turmeric into blender container, cover and blend until smooth. Rub ground mixture well into the fish on both sides. Place fish on 2 or 3 large pieces of banana leaf in a baking dish, sprinkle with chopped coriander and fold leaves over to enclose fish. Secure with bamboo skewers.

Bake in a moderate oven for 35-40 minutes or until fish is cooked. When ready to serve, the flesh will look milky white and flake easily when tested with a fork. Replace banana leaves, lift tish on to a serving plate and open banana leaves at the table.

rendang daging

Dry Fried Beef Curry

Serves: 8

Ingredients	Metric	Imperial
Chuck, blade or round steak	1 kg	2½ lb
Onions, roughly chopped	2 medium	2 medium
Garlic	6 cloves	6 cloves
Chopped fresh root ginger	1 tablespoon	1 tablespoon
Fresh chillies, seeded	6	6
Thick Coconut Milk (see page 66)	100 ml	2 cups
Salt	1½ teaspoons	1½ teaspoons
Ground turmeric	1 teaspoon	1 teaspoon
Chilli powder (optional)	3 teaspoons	3 teaspoons
Ground coriander	2 teaspoons	2 teaspoons
Daun salam leaves	2	2
Dried lemon grass	12 strips	12 strips
Laos powder	1 teaspoon	1 teaspoon
Tamarind liquid	100 ml	½ cup
Sugar	2 teaspoons	2 teaspoons

Cut beef into narrow strips, approximately 5 cm (2-inches) long.

Place onion, garlic, ginger and chillies into blender container with 100 ml (½ cup) of the coconut milk. Cover and blend until smooth, pour into a large saucepan and wash out blender with remaining coconut milk. Add to saucepan with all remaining ingredients except tamarind liquid and sugar. Mix well, add meat and bring quickly to the boil.

Reduce heat to moderate, add tamarind liquid and cook, uncovered, until gravy is thick, stirring occasionally. Turn heat to low and continue cooking until gravy is almost dry, stirring frequently to ensure mixture does not stick to pan. At end of cooking time, approximately 2½ hours, when oil separates from the gravy, add sugar and stir constantly. Allow meat to fry in oil until it is dark brown. Serve with boiled white rice, one or two vegetable dishes, sambals and prawn crisps.

satay manis

Sweet Satay

Serves: 4-6

Ingredients	Metric	Imperial
Fillet steak or pork fillet	600 g	1½ lb
Goela djawa or black sugar	1 tablespoon	1 tablespoon
Garlic, crushed	1 clove	1 clove
Salt	½ teaspoon	½ teaspoon
Soy sauce	2 tablespoons	2 tablespoons
Oil	1 tablespoon	1 tablespoon
Ground cummin	1 teaspoon	1 teaspoon
Satay Sauce:		
Peanut Sauce (see page 75)	100 ml	½ cup
Tamarind liquid or lemon juice	2 tablespoons	2 tablespoons
Sambal badjiak	2 teaspoons	2 teaspoons
Water	3-4 tablespoons	3-4 tablespoons

Cut beef or pork into 2 cm (¾-inch) cubes. Thread 4-5 cubes on each bamboo skewer, not pushing them too close together.

Scrape the cake of goela djawa until you have a tablespoon of shavings. Combine with garlic and salt. Add soy sauce, oil and cummin. Pour into a shallow dish and place the satays in the marinade, turning each one so the marinade coats the meat. Cover and refrigerate for a few hours.

Cook over glowing coals or under a hot grill for approximately 15 minutes, not too close to the source of heat as the pork must be well done. Turn every 5 minutes. Serve hot accompanied with satay sauce.

Satay Sauce: Combine all ingredients and serve in a bowl. The sauce is spooned over the satays before eating.

ajam goreng djawa

Javanese-Style Fried Chicken

Serves: 4-6

Ingredients	Metric	Imperial
Chicken or chicken pieces	1.2 kg	3 lb
Onion, chopped	1 medium	1 medium
Garlic	2 cloves	2 cloves
Finely chopped fresh root ginger	1 teaspoon	1 teaspoon
Fresh chillies or	3	3
sambal oelek (optional)	1 teaspoon	1 teaspoon
Kemiri or brazil nuts	2	2
Coconut Milk (see page 66)	150 ml	¾ cup
Desiccated coconut	1 tablespoon	1 tablespoon
Ground coriander	2 teaspoons	2 teaspoons
Laos (optional)	1 teaspoon	1 teaspoon
Ground turmeric	½ teaspoon	½ teaspoon
Salt	1½ teaspoons	1½ teaspoons
Dried lemon grass (optional)	12 strips	12 strips
Daum salam leaves (optional)	2	2
Oil	for deep frying	for deep frying

Cut chicken into joints—separate drumsticks from thighs, wings from breast and cut breast in half lengthways. (If a whole chicken is used, the back can be cooked in the coconut milk to add flavour, but would not be considered a serving portion.) Chicken pieces most suitable for this dish are breasts or wings. If large, cut breasts into quarters and wings in half.

Place onion, garlic, ginger, chillies and kemiri nuts into blender container with half the coconut milk and desiccated coconut. Cover and blend on high speed for approximately 30 seconds or until smooth. Place blended mixture into a saucepan with the chicken pieces. Wash out blender container with remaining coconut milk and add to pan. Add all remaining ingredients, bring slowly to the boil and cook, uncovered, until chicken is tender and gravy thick and almost dry.

Lift out chicken pieces and deep fry in hot oil until brown, turning occasionally. (A wok or deep frying pan is ideal for this.) Serve with boiled rice or Nasi Goreng (see page 68) and a curry with plenty of gravy.

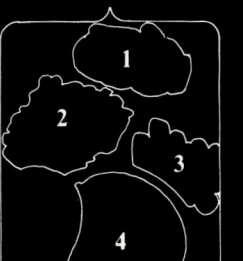

1 country captain
2 spiced spareribs
3 eastern style croquettes
4 mah mi

lay satays
anut sauce

opor ajam

Chicken in Coconut Milk
Serves: 4-6

| Ingredients | Metric | Imperial |

Chicken or chicken pieces	1.2 kg	3 lb
Garlic, crushed	3 cloves	3 cloves
Salt	1 teaspoon	1 teaspoon
Ground black pepper	½ teaspoon	½ teaspoon
Finely grated fresh root ginger	1½ teaspoons	1½ teaspoons
Kemiri or brazil nuts, finely grated	3	3
Ground coriander	3 teaspoons	3 teaspoons
Ground cummin	1 teaspoon	1 teaspoon
Ground fennel (optional)	½ teaspoon	½ teaspoon
Laos (optional)	½ teaspoon	½ teaspoon
Oil	4 tablespoons	4 tablespoons
Onions, finely sliced	2 medium	2 medium
Thin Coconut Milk (see page 66)	400 ml	2 cups
Daun salam leaves	2	2
Dried lemon grass	12 strips	12 strips
Cinnamon stick	5 cm piece	2-inch piece
Thick Coconut Milk (see page 66)	300 ml	1½ cups
Lemon juice or tamarind liquid	1 tablespoon	1 tablespoon
Extra salt	to taste	to taste

Divide chicken into serving pieces. In a small bowl, combine garlic, salt, pepper, ginger, kemiri nuts, coriander, cummin, fennel and laos if used. Mix to a paste, adding a little of the oil if necessary. Rub paste well into the pieces of chicken and leave for 1 hour.

Heat 2 tablespoons of the oil in a frying pan and fry sliced onion slowly until golden brown. Drain from oil and set aside: Add remaining oil to pan and fry the spiced chicken pieces gently, just until they start to colour. Add thin coconut milk, daun salam leaves, lemon grass and cinnamon stick. Stir until it comes to the boil and cook for 30 minutes or until chicken is tender. Add thick coconut milk, stir thoroughly and cook for a further 15 minutes, uncovered. Remove from heat, add lemon juice and season to taste with extra salt. Remove whole spices. Serve with boiled rice, vegetables and sambals.

beef strips, balinese style

Serves: 6

Ingredients	Metric	Imperial
Blade steak	600 g	1½ lb
Onion, roughly chopped	1 medium	1 medium
Garlic	3 cloves	3 cloves
Finely chopped fresh root ginger	1 tablespoon	1 tablespoon
Fresh chillies, seeded	4-6	4-6
Trasi or blachan	½ teaspoon	½ teaspoon
Oil	3 tablespoons	3 tablespoons
Water	200 ml	1 cup
Tamarind liquid	2 tablespoons	2 tablespoons
Soy sauce	2 tablespoons	2 tablespoons
Salt	to taste	to taste

Cut beef into thin strips. Place onion, garlic, ginger, chillies and trasi into blender container, cover and blend until smooth. Heat oil in a saucepan and fry mixture for approximately 5 minutes, stirring constantly. Add beef strips and continue to stir and fry until they change colour. Add water, tamarind liquid and soy sauce, cover and simmer gently until beef is tender. Uncover and cook until liquid has almost evaporated. Season to taste with salt. Serve with boiled white rice, vegetables and sambals.

gado-gado

Cooked Vegetable Salad

Serves: 6-8

Ingredients	Metric	Imperial
Bean sprouts	200 g	8 oz
Cabbage	½ medium	½ medium
Green beans	400 g	1 lb
Tender carrots	3	3
Green cucumber	1	1
Watercress	small bunch	small bunch
Eggs, hard-boiled	3	3
Peanut Sauce (see page 75)		

Wash bean sprouts well, discard any brown 'tails'. Blanch bean sprouts for 1 minute in boiling water. Drain. Shred cabbage coarsely and blanch in boiling salted water for 1-2 minutes, or until tender but still crisp. Drain. String beans and cut in diagonal slices. Cook in boiling salted water for 3 minutes, drain. Wash carrots and cut into thin strips. Cook in lightly salted boiling water until just tender, approximately 5 minutes, drain. Mark skin of cucumber with tines of a fork along the length of it, cut into very thin slices. Wash watercress and break into sprigs. Place crisp watercress sprigs on a plate and on top, arrange the various prepared vegetables separately. Surround with slices of cucumber and place wedges of hard-boiled egg between the different vegetables. Serve with Peanut Sauce.

peanut sauce

There are many recipes for Peanut Sauce, but this is my favourite. Without the addition of liquid, it keeps for weeks in a bottle.

When required, add 3 parts Coconut Milk (see page 66) or water to 1 part sauce and heat. Try it without additional liquid as a sandwich spread, a relish with cold meats or grills, a savoury dip, or a topping for cocktail canapes.

Ingredients	Metric	Imperial
Oil	approximately 7 tablespoons	approximately 7 tablespoons
Dried garlic flakes	1 teaspoon	1 teaspoon
Dried onion flakes	2 tablespoons	2 tablespoons
Dried chillies	2	2
Trasi or blachan	1 teaspoon	1 teaspoon
Lemon juice	1 tablespoon	1 tablespoon
Soy sauce	1 tablespoon	1 tablespoon
Crunchy peanut butter	1x340 g jar	1x12 oz jar
Raw sugar	1½ tablespoons	1½ tablespoons

Heat approximately 1 tablespoon of the oil in a small wok or frying pan and fry garlic flakes for a few seconds until golden. (Oil should not be too hot as they burn easily.) Place on absorbent paper and cool. Heat 2 more tablespoons of the oil and fry onion flakes until golden, drain on absorbent paper and cool. Heat remaining 4 tablespoons oil and fry the dry chillies for approximately 30 seconds until they are puffed and crisp. Remove chillies from pan and cool. Discard stalks and seeds and crumble chillies into small pieces.

In oil remaining in pan (approximately 50 ml (¼ cup), add a little more if necessary) fry trasi mixed with lemon juice and soy sauce. Remove from heat, add peanut butter and stir until well blended. Cool. When quite cold, add crisp garlic and onion flakes, crumbled chillies and sugar. Mix thoroughly and place in a screw-top jar to store.

Use as it is, or mix in enough Coconut Milk (see page 66) or water to make a more liquid consistency, add salt as required.

Note: Fresh garlic and onion may be used instead of dried garlic and onion flakes. Peel 6 garlic cloves and cut into thin slices. Peel and finely slice 1 medium sized onion. Fry separately in approximately 3 tablespoons oil over a low heat, removing from heat as soon as they turn golden brown. Drain on absorbent paper and cool. Crumble the crisp garlic slices before adding to sauce.

malaysia and singapore

Malaysia and Singapore are countries with a cosmopolitan cuisine, mainly Chinese, Indonesian, Indian and the Eastern version of European and American dishes. See, for instance, what native cooks can do with simple fried chicken in the recipe for Country Captain (see page 86).

But Chinese food is what Singapore and Malaysia are famous for. And, or course, the traditional Malay speciality, satay. Street stalls sell an unlimited array of foods and are patronized by rich and poor alike— the appetizing aroma wafting from them is a great leveller!

Maybe it was the appetite brought on by a wild shopping spree in Singapore's duty-free shops that made everything taste so good to me, and most people agree that Singapore is a paradise for lovers of Chinese food.

The food indigenous to South East Asia is characterized by the ever-present prawn paste. In Malaya it is called blachan; in Indonesia, trasi; in Burma, ngapi; in Thailand, kapi. All are made from salted dried prawns, but the end product takes different forms. One variety is very dark brown and hard and sold in flat squares. Another kind comes in cans and this is softer, a greyish-pink in colour. Or it can take the form of a sauce. One thing they all have in common—the smell! But don't be put off by the strong odour. Used in small quantities, this ingredient is what gives the food of South East Asia its distinctive flavour. It keeps indefinitely and if confined in a tightly closed jar it will, like a genie in a bottle, perform its magic on occasion and not obtrude its presence into your kitchen at other times.

malay satay

Ideal for barbecue parties as there is no last minute preparation.

Serves: 8-10

Ingredients	Metric	Imperial
Rump steak	800 g	2 lb
Onion, chopped	1 medium	1 medium
Finely chopped fresh root ginger	1 tablespoon	1 tablespoon
Garlic	3 cloves	3 cloves
Lemon juice or tamarind liquid	1 tablespoon	1 tablespoon
Salt	2 teaspoons	2 teaspoons
Ground coriander	1 tablespoon	1 tablespoon
Ground cummin	1 teaspoon	1 teaspoon
Ground curry leaves	1 teaspoon	1 teaspoon
Ground cardamom	¼ teaspoon	¼ teaspoon
Ground cinnamon	½ teaspoon	½ teaspoon
Ground black pepper	½ teaspoon	½ teaspoon
Ground rice	1 tablespoon	1 tablespoon

Cut steak into small cubes. Place onion, ginger, garlic, lemon juice and salt into blender container, cover and blend on high speed until smooth. Heat coriander and cummin in a dry frying pan until colour darkens slightly, stir or shake constantly to prevent burning. Combine blended mixture, coriander and cummin and remaining ingredients in a mixing bowl. Add meat and rub the mixture well into it. Marinate for at least 1 hour. (If possible, prepare the previous day, cover and refrigerate.)

At serving time, thread meat on bamboo skewers and cook over glowing coals or under a hot grill until meat is tender. Place on a serving plate and serve with Peanut Sauce (see page 75).

savoury rice

Serves: 4

Ingredients	Metric	Imperial
Ghee	2½ tablespoons	2½ tablespoons
Leeks, sliced or	3 large	3 large
shallots, chopped	12	12
Onion, finely sliced	1 medium	1 medium
Fresh chillies, seeded and sliced	2	2
Ham or bacon, chopped	200 g	8 oz
Eggs	6	6
Salt and pepper	to taste	to taste
Cold boiled rice	800 ml	4 cups

Heat ghee and fry leeks, onion, chillies and ham until leeks and onion are golden. Beat eggs with salt and pepper to taste, pour into pan and stir until eggs are creamy and almost set. Add rice and mix thoroughly. Cook, stirring continuously, until heated through.

This is a meal in itself and accompaniments are hardly necessary, but crisp pappadams, Frikkadels (see page 42) and hot pickles or chutneys are suitable to serve with Savoury Rice.

fish in coconut milk

Serves: 2

Ingredients	Metric	Imperial
Spanish mackerel, cod or jewfish steaks	2 large	2 large
Salt	2 teaspoons	2 teaspoons
Ground pepper	½ teaspoon	½ teaspoon
Lemon juice	2 tablespoons	2 tablespoons
Butter	25 g	1 oz
Onion, finely sliced	1 small	1 small
Ground turmeric	¼ teaspoon	¼ teaspoon
Cinnamon stick	2.5 cm piece	1-inch piece
Curry leaves	6	6
Thick Coconut Milk (see page 66)	150 ml	¾ cup
Cornflour	2 teaspoons	2 teaspoons

Wash fish, rub with salt, pepper and lemon juice. Simmer, covered, in very little water in a frying pan for approximately 10 minutes. Lift out on to a serving dish and keep warm. Reserve 150 ml (¾ cup) fish stock.

Heat butter and gently fry onion until soft and golden. Add reserved fish stock, turmeric, cinnamon stick and curry leaves and simmer gently for 10 minutes. Add coconut milk mixed with cornflour and stir over a low heat until sauce thickens. Remove cinnamon stick and curry leaves. Pour sauce over fish and serve with boiled rice.

vindaloo

Vindaloo is an Indian speciality, and the many Indians in Malaya have made this dish a favourite there. Many recipes for Vindaloo include onions, but in this recipe (used by my grandmother) there are none. In India—beef, chicken or pork cooked in this way is preserved without refrigeration.

Serves: 6

Ingredients	Metric	Imperial
Ground cummin	2 tablespoons	2 tablespoons
Black mustard seed	2 tablespoons	2 tablespoons
Chilli powder	1 tablespoon or to taste	1 tablespoon or to taste
Garlic	6 cloves	6 cloves
Finely chopped fresh root ginger	1½ tablespoons	1½ tablespoons
Ground cloves	¼ teaspoon	¼ teaspoon
Ground cardamom	½ teaspoon	½ teaspoon
Ground cinnamon	½ teaspoon	½ teaspoon
Black peppercorns	1 teaspoon	1 teaspoon
Malt vinegar	100 ml	½ cup
Mustard oil	100 ml	½ cup
Salt	2 teaspoons	2 teaspoons
Beef, pork or chicken	800 g	2 lb

Place cummin, mustard seed, chilli powder, garlic, ginger and spices into blender container. Add a little of the malt vinegar, cover and blend until smooth.

Heat mustard oil in a saucepan and when very hot, remove from heat, stir in the ground mixture and then the meat. (Beef and pork should be cut in cubes, chicken in small pieces.) Season to taste with salt. Mix well and stand aside for at least 1 hour. Add remaining vinegar and cook slowly until tender. Serve with boiled rice, vegetables and sambals.

eastern style croquettes

Yield: approximately 18

Ingredients	Metric	Imperial
Oil	2 tablespoons	2 tablespoons
Onion, finely chopped	1 medium	1 medium
Garlic, finely chopped	2 cloves	2 cloves
Finely grated fresh root ginger	½ teaspoon	½ teaspoon
Fresh green chillies, seeded and chopped	2	2
Ground coriander	2 teaspoons	2 teaspoons
Ground cummin	1 teaspoon	1 teaspoon
Minced steak	400 g	1 lb
Salt	1½ teaspoons	1½ teaspoons
Ground black pepper	½ teaspoon	½ teaspoon
Finely chopped fresh coriander	2 tablespoons	2 tablespoons
Shallots, finely chopped	6	6
Potatoes	800 g	2 lb
Extra salt and pepper	to taste	to taste
Egg, beaten	1	1
Fine dry breadcrumbs	for coating	for coating
Oil	for deep frying	for deep frying

Heat oil and gently fry onion, garlic, ginger and chillies until soft. Add coriander, cummin and minced steak and fry, stirring continuously, until meat changes colour. Add salt and pepper, cover and cook until meat is tender. (There should be no liquid left when meat is cooked.) Stir in chopped coriander and allow to cool. When quite cold, mix in shallots.

Cook potatoes in boiling salted water until tender. Drain thoroughly and mash until smooth. Season to taste with salt and pepper. Take 2 tablespoons of mashed potato in one hand, flatten slightly, then place 1 tablespoon of meat mixture in the centre. Mould potato around meat and form into an oval shape. Repeat process until all the meat and potato is used. Dip croquettes in beaten egg, then in breadcrumbs and deep fry in hot oil until golden brown. Drain on absorbent paper and serve hot with Chilli Sauce (see page 86).

spiced spareribs

A favourite recipe because it is so easy and the flavour so special—it may also be prepared a day ahead. When required, grill the spareribs a few minutes on each side, just to heat through. The best way to enjoy spareribs is to pick them up in the fingers.

Serves: 6
Cooking time: 1 hour
Oven temperature: 170-190°C (350-375°F)

Ingredients	Metric	Imperial
Pork spareribs	1.2 kg	3 lb
Garlic	4 cloves	4 cloves
Salt	1½ teaspoons	1½ teaspoons
Ground black pepper	½ teaspoon	½ teaspoon
Five-spice powder	½ teaspoon	½ teaspoon
Honey	1 tablespoon	1 tablespoon
Sesame oil	1 tablespoon	1 tablespoon
Soy sauce	3 tablespoons	3 tablespoons
Hot water	100 ml	½ cup

Separate the spareribs with a sharp knife or ask the butcher to do it for you. Crush garlic with salt, combine with pepper, five-spice powder, honey, sesame oil and soy sauce. Rub well all over the spareribs. Place spareribs in a roasting pan and cook in a moderate oven. After 30 minutes, turn spareribs, add hot water to pan and continue roasting, basting with liquid every 10 minutes, for a further 30 minutes.

Alternatively, heat 1-2 tablespoons peanut oil in a large heavy frying pan and brown spareribs. Add water, cover and simmer for 30-35 minutes or until tender.

Serve hot with boiled rice and plum sauce.

mah mi

Soup Noodles

Serves: 5-6

Ingredients	Metric	Imperial
Raw prawns	400 g	1 lb
Peanut oil	1 tablespoon	1 tablespoon
Water	800 ml	4 cups
Salt	1½ teaspoons	1½ teaspoons
Chicken stock	400 ml	2 cups
Barbecued pork	200 g	8 oz
Bean sprouts	200 g	8 oz
Sesame oil	1 tablespoon	1 tablespoon
Garlic, finely grated	3 cloves	3 cloves
Finely grated fresh root ginger	½ teaspoon	½ teaspoon
Fine egg noodles	100 g	4 oz
Five-spice powder	1 teaspoon	1 teaspoon
Crab meat	1 x 90 g can	1 x 3¼ oz can
Finely chopped shallots	100 ml	½ cup
Cucumber, peeled and diced	1 small	1 small

Shell and de-vein prawns. Wash prawn shells and heads thoroughly, drain. Heat peanut oil in a saucepan and fry heads and shells over a high heat until they turn pink. Add water and salt, cover and cook for 20 minutes. Strain. (If liked, the prawn heads and a little of the stock may be blended for a few seconds in an electric blender, then passed through a fine strainer and the liquid added to the prawn stock. This results in a more flavoursome soup.) Combine prawn and chicken stocks.

Cut barbecued pork into thin slices. Wash and drain bean sprouts. Heat sesame oil and gently fry garlic and ginger. When starting to brown add stock and prawns. Bring to the boil and cook for 5 minutes. Add noodles and cook for a further 5 minutes. Add pork, bean sprouts and five-spice powder, simmer for 2 minutes and serve in a large bowl, garnished with crab meat, shallots and cucumber.

mixed fried vermicelli

Serves: 4-6

Ingredients	Metric	Imperial
Rice vermicelli	200 g	8 oz
Lean pork	200 g	8 oz
Fillet steak	200 g	8 oz
Chicken breast	200 g	8 oz
Raw prawns	200 g	8 oz
Green beans	200 g	8 oz
Bean sprouts	200 g	8 oz
Oil	3 tablespoons	3 tablespoons
Garlic, chopped	3 cloves	3 cloves
Finely grated fresh root ginger	½ teaspoon	½ teaspoon
Shallots, chopped	8	8
Salt	to taste	to taste

Bring a large saucepan of lightly salted water to the boil, add rice vermicelli and return to the boil. Cook for 3 minutes, drain well.

Shred pork, steak and chicken finely. Shell and de-vein prawns. Cut beans into very thin diagonal slices. Wash bean sprouts and remove any discoloured sprouts or brown 'tails'.

Heat oil in a large wok and fry garlic and ginger for a few seconds. Add pork and fry, stirring continuously, for approximately 7 minutes. Add steak, chicken and prawns and fry until they change colour. Add green beans and fry 2 minutes longer, then add bean sprouts and toss together for 1 minute. Finally add shallots and rice vermicelli and toss lightly over a moderate heat until heated through. Serve immediately.

sothi

Coconut Milk Soup

This soup is spooned over boiled rice, not served as a first course by itself.

Serves: 6

Ingredients	Metric	Imperial
Desiccated coconut	200 ml	1 cup
Milk	300 ml	1½ cups
Hot water	500 ml	2½ cups
Onions, sliced	2 medium	2 medium
Curry leaves	6	6
Fresh chillies, seeded	2	2
Ground turmeric	½ teaspoon	½ teaspoon
Salt	1¼ teaspoons	1¼ teaspoons
Prawn powder	2 tablespoons	2 tablespoons
Lemon juice	2 tablespoons	2 tablespoons

Place desiccated coconut and milk in a saucepan and heat gently. Cool to lukewarm and squeeze to extract as much milk as possible (or blend for 1 minute in an electric blender on high speed). Strain through a fine sieve, pressing well with a wooden spoon. Set aside. Repeat process with the same coconut and hot water to extract the thin milk. There should be approximately 500 ml (1 pint) of liquid altogether.

Place thin coconut milk, or second extract, into a saucepan with all other ingredients except thick coconut milk and lemon juice, bring to the boil and simmer for 15 minutes. Add thick coconut milk and heat gently, stirring continuously to prevent soup from curdling. Remove from heat, add lemon juice and stir.

Serve as an accompaniment to boiled rice and a dry curry such as Rendang Daging (see page 70) or Malay Satay (see page 77).

curried cucumbers

Serves: 4-6

Ingredients	Metric	Imperial
Cucumbers	2 large	2 large
Onions, chopped	1 small	1 small
Green chillies, seeded and chopped	2	2
Finely grated fresh root ginger	½ teaspoon	½ teaspoon
Garlic, chopped	2 cloves	2 cloves
Prawn powder	2 teaspoons	2 teaspoons
Ground turmeric	¼ teaspoon	¼ teaspoon
Salt	½ teaspoon	½ teaspoon
Thin Coconut Milk (see page 66)	300 ml	1½ cups
Thick Coconut Milk (see page 66)	100 ml	½ cup
Lemon juice	1 tablespoon	1 tablespoon
Extra salt	to taste	to taste

Peel cucumbers, cut in quarters lengthways, then in small chunks. Place all ingredients except cucumber, thick coconut milk, lemon juice and extra salt into a saucepan and simmer gently until onion is tender. Add cucumber and thick coconut milk and cook, uncovered, for 10 minutes, stirring occasionally. Remove from heat and stir in the lemon juice. Season to taste with extra salt.

fried vegetables

Serves: 4-5

Ingredients	Metric	Imperial
Green beans or zucchini	400 g	1 lb
Onion, chopped	1 medium	1 medium
Garlic	1 clove	1 clove
Blachan	½ teaspoon	½ teaspoon
Kemiri or brazil nuts, chopped	3	3
Chilli powder (optional)	½ teaspoon	½ teaspoon
Oil	2 tablespoons	2 tablespoons
Salt	1 teaspoon or to taste	1 teaspoon or to taste

String beans and cut into halves or cut unpeeled zucchini into chunks. Place onion, garlic, blachan, kemiri nuts and chilli powder if used into blender container, cover and blend until smooth.

Heat oil in a saucepan and fry the blended mixture for approximately 5 minutes. Add vegetables and fry, stirring continuously, until the spice mixture is evenly distributed.

Turn heat to low and cook vegetables until tender but still crisp. Season to taste with salt.

country captain

Serves: 6

Ingredients	Metric	Imperial
Chicken or chicken pieces	1.2 kg	3 lb
Garlic, crushed	2 cloves	2 cloves
Salt	2 teaspoons	2 teaspoons
Ground turmeric	1 teaspoon	1 teaspoon
Ground black pepper	½ teaspoon	½ teaspoon
Oil	4 tablespoons	4 tablespoons
Onions, thinly sliced	4 large	4 large
Fresh red chillies, seeded and sliced	2	2
Water	100 ml	½ cup

Cut chicken into serving pieces. Combine garlic, salt, turmeric and pepper and rub well into chicken. Heat oil in a large saucepan and gently fry half the sliced onion until brown. Remove onion from pan and set aside.

Fry remaining onion and chillies until just starting to colour, then add chicken to pan and fry until golden all over. Add water, cover and simmer gently until chicken is tender. Uncover and continue to simmer, allowing any liquid remaining in pan to evaporate. Serve hot, garnished with the reserved fried onion and accompanied by fried potatoes or Ghee Rice (see page 34).

chilli sauce

This makes a sweet, hot chilli sauce. For a milder flavour, combine with commercial tomato sauce. You can adjust the 'hotness' to suit your own taste, depending on the amount of tomato sauce added.

Ingredients	Metric	Imperial
Chilli powder	100 ml	½ cup
Sugar	600 ml	3 cups
White vinegar	1 x 740 ml bottle	1 x 26 fl oz bottle
Sultanas	300 g	12 oz
Garlic, crushed	8 cloves	8 cloves
Salt	3 teaspoons	3 teaspoons
Finely grated fresh root ginger	1½ teaspoons	1½ teaspoons

Place all ingredients in a large enamel or stainless steel saucepan and bring to the boil. Simmer gently until sultanas are very soft.

Cool, then liquidize in a blender or push through a sieve. Pour into sterilized bottles and seal.

spring rolls

This popular snack is within the scope of any home cook now that the spring roll wrappers or 'skins' or 'shells' as they are called, are available frozen from Chinese grocery stores, approximately 20 in each packet. Thaw before attempting to separate these delicate pastry squares.

Yield: 20

Ingredients	Metric	Imperial
Dried mushrooms	6	6
Peanut oil	3 tablespoons	3 tablespoons
Sesame oil	1 tablespoon	1 tablespoon
Garlic, finely grated	1 clove	1 clove
Finely grated fresh root ginger	½ teaspoon	½ teaspoon
Pork, chopped finely	200 g	8 oz
Raw prawns, de-veined and chopped	200 g	8 oz
Shredded Chinese cabbage (Su Choy)	400 ml	2 cups
Shredded white radish (Rhu Bak)	200 ml	1 cup
Water chestnuts, chopped	12	12
Bamboo shoots, chopped	200 ml	1 cup
Bean sprouts	100 g	4 oz
Shallots, finely chopped	6	6
Soy sauce	1 tablespoon	1 tablespoon
Oyster sauce	1 tablespoon	1 tablespoon
Salt	1 teaspoon	1 teaspoon
Cornflour	3 teaspoons	3 teaspoons
Frozen spring roll wrappers	1 packet	1 packet
Oil	for deep frying	for deep frying

Cover mushrooms with hot water and soak for 20 minutes. Remove stalks and chop mushrooms. Heat peanut and sesame oil in a wok and slowly fry garlic and ginger for a few seconds. Add pork and fry until it changes colour. Add prawns and continue stirring and frying until they are cooked. Add prepared vegetables, soy sauce, oyster sauce and salt, combine thoroughly. Push mixture to one side and tilt wok so liquid gathers. Stir in cornflour which has been mixed with a little cold water until smooth. Cook, stirring continuously, until thick. Remove wok from heat and mix thickened liquid through the filling. Allow to cool completely.

Place 2 tablespoons of the mixture at one end of each spring roll wrapper and roll up, turning in the sides so that filling is completely enclosed. Dampen edges with water or a mixture of cornflour and water and press to seal.

Fry one or two at a time in deep hot oil until golden brown. Drain on absorbent paper and serve immediately, with Chilli Sauce (see page 86) if desired.

agar-agar jelly

Serves: 6

Ingredients	Metric	Imperial
Water	1.2 litres	6 cups
Agar-agar powder	4 teaspoons	4 teaspoons
Sugar	200 ml	1 cup
Red colouring	few drops	few drops
Rose essence	3-4 drops	3-4 drops
Vanilla essence	½ teaspoon	½ teaspoon
Green colouring	few drops	few drops
Almond essence	3-4 drops	3-4 drops

Pour water into a saucepan, sprinkle with agar-agar powder and bring slowly to the boil. Boil until agar dissolves, 5-10 minutes. Add sugar and stir over heat until it dissolves. Remove from heat, pour 400 ml (2 cups) of the jelly into a bowl, colour pink with red colouring and flavour with rose essence. Pour into a chilled mould, previously rinsed with cold water and set in the refrigerator. Keep remaining jelly warm in a pan of hot water.

As soon as the first layer sets (this takes only a few minutes) pour 400 ml (2 cups) more agar mixture into the bowl and flavour with vanilla. Pour gently over the first layer and chill. Repeat with remaining jelly, colouring it a pale shade of green with green colouring and flavouring with almond essence. Chill until serving time.

Unmould on to a serving plate and serve with custard or ice cream.

Note: Agar-agar powder may be purchased from chemists or Chinese grocery stores.

cold hors d'oeuvre

chicken with walnuts and broccoli
plain white rice

china and japan

Chinese cooking is one of the great cuisines of the world.

The food of China can be delicate, as in the Peking or Shantung school of cooking; hot and spicy as in Szechuanese food; spicy, sweet and sour, Honan style; subtle, as in the school of Fukien, famous for its clear soups and seafood dishes; or a combination of many styles as in Cantonese cooking. Cantonese food is the most popular in the West.

Cooking Chinese food is not difficult. But remember that all preparation must be done before cooking starts. Meat, poultry and vegetables are diced, sliced or shredded and seasonings measured out, because there is no time to do this once the heat is on—literally. The cooking itself takes only a few minutes.

Stir-frying is an essential technique in Chinese cooking—it is to stir and toss ingredients vigorously in very little oil over a high heat. (This is easy to do in a Chinese wok. These pans are readily available.)

Ingredients are added in a certain order—those which take longest to cook being put in first. With a little practice, this split-second timing becomes second nature.

It is better to let guests wait for a Chinese meal because if the food has to wait even a few minutes it will continue cooking in its own heat and the effect will be spoilt.

Vegetables should be tender but still crisp. Meat, chicken, pork and seafood must be well cooked but never overdone or dry.

A Chinese meal does not feature one main dish. It is a succession of courses, but as always in Eastern food, the foundation of the meal is rice. Desserts are not a feature of Chinese meals.

Japanese food is very light and delicate. It is also very beautiful to look at, and good cooks are artists in the arrangement of food. Again, rice cooked the Oriental way is the essential item.

Two popular Japanese dishes are Beef Teriyaki and Shabu-Shabu, and both are cooked at the table. What better way to combine good food and good conversation? Maybe you will decide to serve one of these dishes at your next dinner party.

China
cold hors d'oeuvre

Serves: 6-8

Ingredients	Metric	Imperial
Abalone	1 x 455 g can	1x1 lb can
Braized Mushrooms (see page 98)	½ quantity	½ quantity
Barbecued pork	200 g	8 oz
Cooked chicken breast	1	1
Dried red Chinese sausages	2 pairs	2 pairs
Tea Eggs, quartered (see below)	6	6
Cucumber, thinly sliced	1 large	1 large
White radish, thinly sliced	1 large	1 large
Marinade:		
Soy sauce	4 tablespoons	4 tablespoons
Sugar	1 tablespoon	1 tablespoon
Sherry	1 tablespoon	1 tablespoon
Sesame oil	1 tablespoon	1 tablespoon
Finely grated fresh root ginger	½ teaspoon	½ teaspoon

Drain abalone and discard liquid from can. Cut abalone into very thin slices and place in marinade. Slice braized mushrooms thinly. Cut barbecued pork and chicken breast in thin slices. Steam sausages for 10 minutes or until plump, cool and cut in paper-thin diagonal slices. Drain the abalone slices and reserve the marinade.

Arrange ingredients attractively on a large serving plate and serve marinade in a small bowl as a dip.

Marinade: Mix all ingredients together thoroughly.

tea eggs

Place 6 eggs in a saucepan, cover with cold water and bring slowly to the boil, stirring gently. (This helps to centre the yolks.) Simmer gently for 7 minutes. Cool eggs thoroughly under running cold water for 5 minutes. Lightly crack each egg shell by rolling on a hard surface. Shell should be cracked all over, but do not remove.

Bring 800 ml (4 cups) water to the boil, add 3 tablespoons tea leaves, 1 tablespoon salt and 1 teaspoon five-spice powder. Add cracked eggs. Simmer, covered, for approximately 30 minutes or until shells turn brown. Let eggs stand in covered pan for 30 minutes (or longer, overnight if possible.) Drain, cool and shell. The whites of eggs will have a marbled pattern on them.

crab and egg soup

Serves: 5

Ingredients	Metric	Imperial
Chicken stock	1.2 litres	6 cups
Crab meat	2x185 g cans	2x6½ oz cans
Eggs, slightly beaten	3	3
Cornflour	2 tablespoons	2 tablespoons
Cold water	50 ml	¼ cup
Shallots, finely sliced	6	6
Chopped fresh coriander (optional)	2 tablespoons	2 tablespoons

Bring chicken stock to the boil. Drain and flake crab meat, picking out and discarding any bony tissue. Add to stock. Return stock to the boil and add the slightly beaten eggs very slowly. Do not stir. After 2 minutes, stir in the cornflour mixed to a smooth paste with the cold water. Return soup to the boil, stirring constantly.

Remove from heat, sprinkle with shallots and coriander if used and serve immediately in deep bowls.

prawn ball soup

Serves: 4-6

Ingredients	Metric	Imperial
Prawn Balls:		
Raw prawns, shelled and de-veined	400 g	1 lb
Water chestnuts	5	5
Garlic, crushed	1 clove	1 clove
Finely grated fresh root ginger	½ teaspoon	½ teaspoon
Salt	1 teaspoon	1 teaspoon
Shallots, finely chopped	5	5
Chopped fresh coriander	2 tablespoons	2 tablespoons
Soft white bread, crumbled	1 slice	1 slice
Egg-yolk	1	1
Cornflour	1 teaspoon	1 teaspoon
Soup:		
Fine egg noodles	50 g	2 oz
Peanut oil	2 tablespoons	2 tablespoons
Garlic, finely chopped	2 cloves	2 cloves
Water and chicken stock cubes	1 litre	5 cups
Cornflour	2 teaspoons	2 teaspoons
Tender Chinese cabbage, finely sliced	6 leaves	6 leaves
Shallots, cut in 2.5 cm (1-inch) lengths	6	6

Prawn Balls. Chop prawns very finely. Chop water chestnuts in small pieces. Combine all ingredients thoroughly and form into small balls.

Soup: Cook noodles in boiling salted water until just tender. Drain. Heat oil in a large saucepan and gently fry garlic until soft. Add stock and bring to the boil. Add prawn balls, dropping them into the boiling stock one at a time, and cook gently for approximately 8-10 minutes. Blend cornflour until smooth with a little water. Add to soup and cook 1 minute longer. Remove from heat, add cabbage, shallots and noodles. Mix thoroughly and serve immediately.

special fried rice

Serves: 6
or 8-10 as an accompaniment

Ingredients	Metric	Imperial
Short grain rice	800 g	2 lb
Dried Chinese mushrooms	50 g	2 oz
Dried red Chinese sausages	2 pairs	2 pairs
Barbecued pork	200 g	8 oz
Green beans	200 g	8 oz
Celery	3 stalks	3 stalks
Peanut oil	4 tablespoons	4 tablespoons
Sesame oil	2 tablespoons	2 tablespoons
Finely grated fresh root ginger	1½ teaspoons	1½ teaspoons
Garlic, finely chopped	2 cloves	2 cloves
Cooked small prawns, shelled and de-veined	400 g	1 lb
Chopped shallots	300 ml	1½ cups
Chicken stock or reserved mushroom liquid	100 ml	½ cup
Soy sauce	3 tablespoons	3 tablespoons
Monosodium glutamate (optional)	½ teaspoon	½ teaspoon
Salt	to taste	to taste

Cook rice (see page 67), the day before required and allow to cool. With the fingers, separate grains and refrigerate overnight. Soak mushrooms in hot water for 20 minutes. Drain and reserve liquid. Cut off stems with a sharp knife and discard, slice mushrooms thinly. Steam sausages in a colander over boiling water for 5-10 minutes until they are plump. On a wooden board, using a sharp Chinese chopper, cut sausages diagonally into paper-thin slices. Thinly slice barbecued pork. String beans and celery and cut into very thin diagonal slices.

Heat peanut and sesame oil in a large wok, add ginger and garlic and stir-fry for 30 seconds. Add mushrooms, beans and celery and stir-fry over a high heat for a further 3 minutes. Add sausage, pork and prawns and heat. Add rice and continue tossing mixture until rice is heated through. Add shallots.

Mix chicken stock or reserved mushroom liquid with soy sauce and monosodium glutamate if used. Sprinkle evenly over rice and mix well. Season to taste with salt.

fireworks prawns

Serves: 6

Ingredients	Metric	Imperial
Raw prawns	400 g	1 lb
Bacon	6 rashers	6 rashers
Oil	2 tablespoons	2 tablespoons
Onion, finely chopped	1 medium	1 medium
Garlic, finely chopped	3 cloves	3 cloves
Finely grated fresh root ginger	2 teaspoons	2 teaspoons
Fresh red chillies, seeded and finely sliced	3	3
Chilli Sauce (see page 86)	2 tablespoons	2 tablespoons
Tomato purée or tomato sauce	100 ml	½ cup
Chinese wine or sherry	2 tablespoons	2 tablespoons
Oyster sauce	1 tablespoon	1 tablespoon
Soy sauce	1 tablespoon	1 tablespoon
Honey	1 tablespoon	1 tablespoon
Vinegar	1 tablespoon	1 tablespoon
Monosodium glutamate	¼ teaspoon	¼ teaspoon
Salt	¼ teaspoon	¼ teaspoon
Shallots, cut in 5 cm (2-inch) lengths	8	8
Oil	for deep frying	for deep frying
Batter:		
Eggs	2	2
Plain flour or cornflour	100 ml	½ cup
Salt	½ teaspoon	½ teaspoon

Shell prawns, leaving tails on. De-vein, then split prawns with tip of a sharp knife, about half way through, and open out flat. Press with palm of hand. Remove rind from bacon and cut each rasher into pieces approximately the same size as the prawns. Place a piece of bacon on each prawn.

Heat oil and gently fry onion, garlic, ginger and chillies until onion is soft and golden. Add Chilli Sauce, tomato purée, wine, oyster sauce, soy sauce, honey, vinegar, monosodium glutamate and salt. Stir well and remove from heat. Add shallots.

Heat oil in a wok or frying pan. Dip each prawn together with piece of bacon in batter, then drop immediately into hot oil and deep fry until golden and crisp. Drain on absorbent paper, arrange on a plate and spoon sauce over. Serve immediately.

Batter: Sieve flour and salt into a mixing bowl. Make a well in the centre, add eggs and beat ingredients together until batter is smooth.

barbecued loin of pork

Serves: 6-7
Cooking time: approximately 1½ hours
Oven temperature: 230-260°C (450-500°F)
reducing to 160-170°C (325-350 F)

Ingredients	Metric	Imperial
Loin of pork	1.2 kg	3 lb
Garlic, crushed	4 cloves	4 cloves
Finely grated fresh root ginger	2 teaspoons	2 teaspoons
Hoy sin sauce	2 tablespoons	2 tablespoons
Honey	3 tablespoons	3 tablespoons
Soy sauce	4 tablespoons	4 tablespoons
Five-spice powder	1 teaspoon	1 teaspoon
Sesame seeds (optional)	2 tablespoons	2 tablespoons
Hot water	200 ml	1 cup
Cold water	6 tablespoons	6 tablespoons

Ask the butcher to score skin of pork very lightly and to separate the chops without cutting through the skin and the fat underneath. Mix remaining ingredients together except hot and cold water. Place pork, skin side down, in a roasting pan. Spoon approximately half the marinade over, making sure it goes between each chop. Rub marinade well over all the cut surfaces and stand aside for at least 1 hour. Turn pork over so skin is uppermost and place on a rack in the roasting pan. Wipe any traces of marinade from skin with a damp paper towel, then dry the skin well. Pour hot water into pan, being careful not to pour it over pork.

Place pork in a very hot oven for 30 minutes, then reduce oven heat to moderately slow. Continue cooking pork for a further 30 minutes. Remove rack from pan, turn pork over and continue cooking for a further 30 minutes or until tender, basting every 10 minutes with fat and marinade in pan.

Add cold water to remaining marinade and simmer in a small saucepan for 5 minutes. Serve pork hot, with extra marinade in a small bowl for dipping or pouring over pork.

chicken with cashew nuts and snow peas

In a quickly cooked dish like this one, the flexibility of gas heat is desirable, but if using an electric stove, preheat the hot plate until the high heat required is obtained, then lift pan on and off hot plate as more or less heat is required.

Serves: 6

Ingredients	Metric	Imperial
Chicken breasts	300 g	1½ lb
Cornflour or chestnut flour	3 teaspoons	3 teaspoons
Five-spice powder	½ teaspoon	½ teaspoon
Salt	½ teaspoon	½ teaspoon
Oil	for deep frying	for deep frying
Raw cashew nuts	200 ml	1 cup
Extra oil	4 tablespoons	4 tablespoons
Snow peas	100 g	4 oz
Finely grated fresh root ginger	1½ teaspoons	1½ teaspoons
Garlic, crushed	1 small clove	1 small clove
Chinese wine or sherry	2 tablespoons	2 tablespoons
Soy sauce	1 tablespoon	1 tablespoon
Sugar	1 teaspoon	1 teaspoon
Cornflour	2 teaspoons	2 teaspoons
Cold water	2 tablespoons	2 tablespoons

Bone chicken breasts and cut flesh into small pieces, approximately 1 cm (½-inch) square. Sieve cornflour, five-spice powder and salt over chicken pieces and mix well. Set aside. Heat oil and deep fry cashew nuts over a moderate heat until golden. Lift out and drain on absorbent paper.

Heat 2 tablespoons of the extra oil in a wok and quickly stir-fry the snow peas over a high heat for 30 seconds, just until they turn a deeper green. Lift on to a plate. Add remaining extra oil to wok, fry ginger and garlic for a few seconds, then add chicken and fry, stirring continuously, over a high heat until chicken changes colour. (This will only take a minute or two.) Add remaining ingredients mixed together and stir over heat until liquid boils and thickens. Remove from heat, mix in cashew nuts and snow peas and serve immediately.

chicken with walnuts and broccoli

Make Chicken with Cashew Nuts and Snow Peas (see page 96) but substitute an equal quantity of tender broccoli (or thinly sliced green beans) for snow peas. They should be fried for approximately 3 minutes. Substitute peeled walnuts for cashew nuts.

chicken livers with vegetables

Serves: 3-4

Ingredients	Metric	Imperial
Chicken livers	200 g	8 oz
Cornflour	2 teaspoons	2 teaspoons
Salt	½ teaspoon	½ teaspoon
Five-spice powder	½ teaspoon	½ teaspoon
Peanut oil	2 tablespoons	2 tablespoons
Garlic, finely grated	1 clove	1 clove
Finely grated fresh root ginger	½ teaspoon	½ teaspoon
Finely sliced Chinese cabbage	800 ml	4 cups
Shallots, cut into 5 cm (2-inch) lengths	6	6
Soy sauce	1 tablespoon	1 tablespoon
Water	4 tablespoons	4 tablespoons
Extra cornflour	2 teaspoons	2 teaspoons
Monosodium glutamate	¼ teaspoon	¼ teaspoon

Wash chicken livers. Cut in halves and then in quarters, removing any tubes and membranes. Place on absorbent paper to drain. Combine cornflour, salt and five-spice powder and dust over chicken livers.

Heat oil, add garlic and ginger and stir for a few seconds. Add chicken livers and fry, stirring continuously over a moderate heat, for 2-3 minutes. Add vegetables and stir-fry 1 minute longer. Mix soy sauce, water, extra cornflour and monosodium glutamate together until smooth. Add to pan and stir over heat 1 minute longer or until liquid boils and thickens. Serve immediately over boiled or fried noodles.

braized mushrooms

Serves: 6-8

Ingredients	Metric	Imperial
Dried Chinese mushrooms	100 g	4 oz
Hot water	600-800 ml	3-4 cups
Soy sauce	2 tablespoons	2 tablespoons
Sugar	2 tablespoons	2 tablespoons
Sesame oil	1 tablespoon	1 tablespoon
Monosodium glutamate (optional)	¼ teaspoon	¼ teaspoon
Peanut oil	3 tablespoons	3 tablespoons

Wash mushrooms well in cold water. Place in a bowl and pour over hot water. Allow to soak for 20 minutes. With a sharp knife, cut stems off and discard. Squeeze as much water as possible from the mushrooms, reserving the liquid. To the reserved liquid, add some of the water in which the mushrooms were soaked, enough to make 300 ml (1½ cups). Add the soy sauce, sugar, sesame oil and monosodium glutamate if used. Stir to dissolve sugar.

Heat peanut oil in a small wok and fry mushrooms over a high heat, stirring and turning, until the undersides are browned. Add liquid mixture, lower heat, cover and simmer for approximately 30 minutes or until all the liquid is absorbed and the mushrooms take on a shiny appearance. Towards the end of cooking time, it is advisable to stir occasionally. Serve hot or cold.

Note: Braized Mushrooms may also be added to other dishes, either whole or sliced.

Japan
shabu-shabu

Shabu-Shabu is the Japanese version of Mongolian Fire Pot or Singapore Steamboat. Guests cook their own meal at the table, holding pieces of steak and vegetables with chopsticks and dipping them into boiling stock. The name actually comes from the gentle swishing sound made as the food is cooked.

Serves: 6-8

Ingredients	Metric	Imperial
Fillet steak	1 kg	2½ lb
Chinese mustard cabbage	1	1
Shallots	1 bunch	1 bunch
Carrots	2	2
Button mushrooms	400 g	1 lb
Chicken stock or water and chicken stock cubes	2 litres or more	10 cups or more
Sesame Seed Sauce:		
Sesame seeds	2 tablespoons	2 tablespoons
Vinegar	1 tablespoon	1 tablespoon
Light soy sauce	6 tablespoons	6 tablespoons
Finely chopped shallot	2 tablespoons	2 tablespoons
Finely grated fresh root ginger	1 teaspoon	1 teaspoon

Cut steak in very thin slices. (It is easier to do this if you partially freeze the meat, slice while frozen, then thaw in the refrigerator.)

Cut cabbage into short lengths, using stems and only the base of the leaves. Cut shallots into bite-size lengths. Cut carrots in round slices, parboil and drain. Wipe mushrooms with a damp cloth, trim ends of stalks and cut in halves.

At serving time, pour stock to a depth of at least 2.5 cm (1-inch) in a table-top cooker or electric frypan. Heat and place in the centre of the table, within easy reach of everyone. Keep stock boiling throughout the meal, adding more as necessary. Serve sauce in small individual bowls. Supply guests with bowls to eat from, sauce bowls, chopsticks and spoons. Also serve a large bowl of boiled white rice so guests can help themselves.

Pick up raw ingredients with chopsticks and hold them in the boiling stock briefly, until just done. Care should be taken not to overcook them. Steak should be pale pink when cooked and vegetables tender but still crisp. Steak and vegetables are dipped into the sauce and eaten immediately. When all the meat and vegetables are eaten, the stock is served as a soup.

Sesame Seed Sauce: Lightly brown sesame seeds in a dry pan, stirring over a moderate heat. Crush with a mortar and pestle. Combine with remaining ingredients.

beef teriyaki

Serves: 4

Ingredients	Metric	Imperial
Fillet steak	600 g	1½ lb
Finely grated fresh root ginger	2 teaspoons	2 teaspoons
Garlic, crushed	1 clove	1 clove
Soy sauce	100 ml	½ cup
Mirin or sherry	2 tablespoons	2 tablespoons
Sugar	1 tablespoon	1 tablespoon
Sesame oil	1 tablespoon	1 tablespoon
Cornflour	2 teaspoons	2 teaspoons

Cut fillet into thin steaks. Mix all remaining ingredients together except cornflour and marinate the steak for at least 2 hours. Heat griller, hibachi or electric frypan. Before starting to cook the meat, mix 2 tablespoons of the marinade with an equal quantity of water. Mix cornflour to a smooth paste with a little of the mixture. Bring remaining mixture to the boil and stirring continuously, add the blended cornflour and cook until clear and thickened. Set aside.

Grill or fry slices of steak for a few minutes on each side. Pour a spoonful of the glaze on each one and cut in strips before serving, (to facilitate eating with chopsticks). Serve with boiled white rice.

entertaining

One of the best ways to give a dinner party with comparatively little last-minute effort is to make it a curry meal. Exotic, authentic curries are popular with just about everyone and are actually improved by being made a day or two in advance, cooled quickly and refrigerated. Flavours develop and blend and the curry tastes even better than when it is freshly made.

The complete menu can be Eastern, from hors d'oeuvre to dessert. Set the mood with a tablecloth of printed fabric in vibrant Eastern colours, a low float-bowl of frangipani or other flowers, candles or oil lamps, large brass or copper trays.

A barefoot Indian bearer in white coat and dhoti to serve the food would be the perfect finishing touch, but you can't buy them at the supermarket so concentrate instead on the most important thing, the food itself.

A really good curry meal is an experience gourmets remember with pleasure. There is an art to making good curry, but it is an easy one to learn. Just follow the recipes in this book and don't be tempted to throw in other ingredients. I have learned, I think, not to show my feelings when curry enthusiasts assure me they make a really good curry with 'everything' in it, and proceed to enumerate the 'chopped apples and bananas, sultanas and currants'. These fruits may be used as accompaniments, but please, not *in* the curry!

Curries don't have to be hot. So many spices, herbs and aromatic seeds go into the flavouring of curries, that if a mild curry is preferred, just leave out the chilli or pepper. The result will still be fragrant, appetizing and authentic.

What drinks to serve with a curry meal? This is a much debated question. In curry eating countries plain cold water is always on the table or, sometimes, ice-cold fruit juice or sherbet. This is not a frozen sherbet but a sweet, highly-flavoured cordial mixed with either water or milk, and crushed ice.

Many people prefer to have an alchoholic beverage and a good lager is very compatible with highly spiced curries. A sweet spiced wine punch may also be served but wines, especially fine dry wines, do not compliment the flavour of curry. Neither does a curry help the taste of a fine wine. Each is beautiful in its own way but they are best enjoyed at different times.

I have planned a dinner party for 8-10 people, a buffet dinner for 10-12 and a large buffet for approximately 25. One of the nice things about Eastern meals is the flexibility where extra guests are concerned—curries stretch so easily.

I hope that at this point you are already reaching for pad and pencil to make up a guest list. And as you relax and enjoy your own party, you'll bless the make-ahead recipes that take the headache out of hostessing. May your guests always be as appreciative as mine are.

> **Dinner party for 8-10**
> Cocktail Savouries
> Mulligatawny
> Rice Vermicelli Pilau
> Spicy Fried Chicken
> Prawn Coconut Curry (see page 37)
> Chilli Sambol (see page 44)
> Fried Eggplant Sambol (see page 47)
> Vattalappam (see page 48)

cocktail savouries

With pre-dinner drinks serve either Samoosas (see page 26) or crisp pappadam strips. Buy a packet of pappadams and cut each one with a sharp knife into 4 strips. Deep fry in very hot oil, two or three at a time, for just a few seconds. They will swell and turn golden immediately they are dropped into the oil. Drain on absorbent paper and serve hot. If preferred, they may be fried an hour or so beforehand, cooled, then stored in an airtight container.

mulligatawny

The curry-flavoured soup derives its name from the Indian 'mulegoo-thani' or pepper water. (Mulegoo means pepper, thani means water.) In South India, pepper water appears on the table at almost every meal as it contains ingredients that aid the digestion. It is simply and cheaply made with water instead of stock.

Mulligatawny may be made with beef, chicken or fish stock and this recipe includes coconut milk, which gives it richness and delicious flavour.

Ingredients	Metric	Imperial
Gravy beef	800 g	2 lb
Soup bones	800 g	2 lb
Onion	1	1
Cloves	3	3
Cardamom pods	6	6
Curry leaves	1 tablespoon	1 tablespoon
Coriander seeds	2 tablespoons	2 tablespoons
Cummin seeds	1 tablespoon	1 tablespoon
Garlic	3 cloves	3 cloves
Black peppercorns	12	12
Salt	2 teaspoons	2 teaspoons
Tamarind pulp (optional)	1 tablespoon	1 tablespoon
For Finishing:		
Ghee	1 tablespoon	1 tablespoon
Onions, finely sliced	2	2
Black mustard seed	½ teaspoon	½ teaspoon
Curry leaves	8	8
Coconut Milk (see page 66)	600 ml	3 cups
Salt	to taste	to taste

Place beef and bones in a large saucepan with sufficient water to cover. Add whole onion studded with cloves, cardamom pods, curry leaves, coriander and cummin seeds, garlic, peppercorns, salt and tamarind pulp if used.

Bring to the boil, reduce heat and simmer gently for 1½-2 hours or until beef is tender and stock is reduced. Cool slightly.

Remove beef and bones from stock, discard bones. Cut beef into small dice and reserve. Pour stock through a fine strainer. (There should be approximately 1.2 litres (6 cups) of stock.)

To Finish: Heat ghee and fry finely sliced onion until dark brown. Add mustard seed and curry leaves and stir a minute or two. Pour hot stock into pan. (It will hiss and spit, so be careful.)

Simmer for 5 minutes. Just before serving, add coconut milk. Season to taste with salt. If tamarind pulp is not used, add lemon juice to taste, approximately 2 tablespoons. Return diced beef to pan. Heat but do not boil. Serve hot.

Note: Contrary to popular belief, boiled rice is not always served with Mulligatawny. When a main course of rice or other starchy food is to follow, it is definitely left out.

rice vermicelli pilau

Ingredients	Metric	Imperial
Rice vermicelli	400 g	1 lb
Ghee	5 tablespoons	5 tablespoons
Onions, finely sliced	3 large	3 large
Curry leaves	10	10
Powdered saffron or saffron strands	1 good pinch ½ teaspoon	1 good pinch ½ teaspoon
Ground turmeric	1 teaspoon	1 teaspoon
Ground cardamom	1 teaspoon	1 teaspoon
Salt and pepper	to taste	to taste
Eggs, hard-boiled	4-5	4-5
Peas, cooked	200 ml	1 cup
Cashew nuts or almonds, fried until golden brown in oil	50 ml	¼ cup

Cook rice vermicelli in a large quantity of lightly salted boiling water for 3 minutes, no longer. Drain in a large colander.

Heat ghee in a large saucepan and fry onion and curry leaves until onion is golden. Add saffron, turmeric and cardamom and stir well. Add rice vermicelli and toss ingredients together until well mixed and evenly coloured. Season to taste with salt and pepper.

Serve garnished with eggs cut into slices or quarters, peas and nuts.

Note: If liked, the hard-boiled eggs may be rubbed with ground turmeric and fried in a little hot oil until golden.

ikan bandeng

chinese ingredients

1 chinese cabbage
2 cellophane noodles
3 rice vermicelli
4 abalone
5 bamboo shoots
6 fresh bean sprouts
7 chinese chopper
8 soy sauce
9 oyster sauce
10 sesame oil
11 shallots
12 long white radishes
13 dried mushrooms
14 fresh root ginger
15 garlic
16 wide egg noodles
17 fine egg noodles
18 fresh coriander
19 peeled walnuts
20 fresh water chestnuts
21 star anise
22 5-spice powder
23 canned water chestnuts
24 red chinese sausages

spicy fried chicken

Ingredients	Metric	Imperial
Chickens	2x1.2 kg	2x3 lb
Garlic, crushed	3 cloves	3 cloves
Finely grated fresh root ginger	1½ teaspoons	1½ teaspoons
Ghee, melted	1 tablespoon	1 tablespoon
Ground turmeric	1 teaspoon	1 teaspoon
Ground rice	2 teaspoons	2 teaspoons
Soy sauce	2 teaspoons	2 teaspoons
Ground coriander	2 teaspoons	2 teaspoons
Garam masala	1 teaspoon	1 teaspoon
Ground cummin	1 teaspoon	1 teaspoon
Salt	2 teaspoons	2 teaspoons
Pepper	½ teaspoon	½ teaspoon
Oil	for frying	for frying

Cut chickens into serving pieces. Detach wings from breasts and cut breasts in two. Separate thighs from drumsticks and discard backs. Combine all remaining ingredients except oil and rub well all over the pieces of chicken. Marinate for at least 1 hour, refrigerate overnight if possible.

Heat oil in a large frying pan and fry chicken pieces over a moderate heat until golden brown, allow approximately 10 minutes on each side. Drain on absorbent paper.

To keep hot, place chicken pieces in a baking dish, cover with aluminium foil and place in a very slow oven 120°C (250°F).

Note: I also like to prepare this using only chicken drumsticks. Allow 2 drumsticks for each person.

prawn coconut curry

Follow Prawn Coconut Curry recipe on page 37, increasing quantity of prawns to 1-2 kg (3lb).

> **Buffet Party for 10-12**
> Pakorhas (see page 28) or Singaras (see page 27)
> Frikkadels (see page 42)
> Pork Badun (see page 40) double quantity
> Muslim Style Chicken Biriani
> Onion Sambal (see page 25) double quantity
> Cucumber Salad (see page 24) double quantity
> Falooda

muslim style chicken biriani

For Biriani, always use long grain rice. Basmati rice with its thin, fine grains is the ideal variety to use in this festive dish. This quantity will serve 12 and is ideal for a special party, but if you want to experiment for a small number, simply halve the quantities but keep cooking times the same.

Ingredients	Metric	Imperial
Chicken Savoury:		
Chickens	2x1.2 kg	2x3 lb
Ghee	10 tablespoons	10 tablespoons
Blanched almonds	4 tablespoons	4 tablespoons
Sultanas	4 tablespoons	4 tablespoons
New potatoes	8 small	8 small
Onions, finely chopped	4 large	4 large
Garlic, finely chopped	10 cloves	10 cloves
Finely chopped fresh root ginger	1½ tablespoons	1½ tablespoons
Chilli powder	1 teaspoon	1 teaspoon
Ground pepper	1 teaspoon	1 teaspoon
Ground turmeric	1 teaspoon	1 teaspoon
Ground cummin	2 teaspoons	2 teaspoons
Salt	2 teaspoons	2 teaspoons
Tomatoes, peeled and chopped	3 large	3 large
Yoghurt	4 tablespoons	4 tablespoons
Chopped mint	4 tablespoons	4 tablespoons
Ground cardamom	1 teaspoon	1 teaspoon
Cinnamon stick	8 cm piece	3-inch piece

<u>Biriani Rice:</u>

Basmati rice	1 litre	5 cups
Ghee	5 tablespoons	5 tablespoons
Onions, finely chopped	2 large	2 large
Powdered saffron or	2 good pinches	2 good pinches
saffron strands	½ teaspoon	½ teaspoon
Cardamom pods	10	10
Cloves	6	6
Cinnamon stick	2.5 cm piece	1-inch piece
Powdered aromatic ginger	1 teaspoon	1 teaspoon
Rose water	4 tablespoons	4 tablespoons
Salt	3 teaspoons	3 teaspoons
Strong chicken stock or water and chicken stock cubes	1.6 litres	8 cups

<u>Chicken Savoury:</u> Cut chickens into serving pieces. Heat half the ghee in a small frying pan, fry almonds until they are golden, drain. Fry sultanas for a few seconds and set aside. Fry peeled and halved potatoes until they are brown, drain and reserve.

Pour any ghee left in frying pan into a large saucepan, add remaining ghee and heat. Fry onion, garlic and ginger until onion is soft and golden. Add chilli powder, pepper, turmeric, cummin, salt and tomato. Fry, stirring continuously, for 5 minutes. Add yoghurt, mint, cardamom and cinnamon stick. Cover and cook over a low heat, stirring occasionally, until tomato is cooked to a pulp. (It may be necessary to add a little hot water if mixture becomes too dry and starts to stick to pan.) When mixture is thick and smooth, add chicken pieces and stir well to coat them with spice mixture. Cover and cook over a very low heat until chicken is tender, approximately 35-45 minutes. There should be only a little very thick gravy when chicken is cooked. If necessary, cook uncovered for a few minutes to reduce gravy.

<u>Biriani Rice:</u> Wash rice well and drain in colander for at least 30 minutes. Heat ghee and fry onion until golden. Add saffron, cardamom pods, cloves, cinnamon stick, aromatic ginger and rice. Fry, stirring continuously until rice is coated with the ghee. Add rose water and salt to hot stock, pour over rice mixture and stir well. Add chicken savoury and potatoes and gently mix into the rice.

Cover saucepan tightly, turn heat to very low and steam for 20 minutes. Do not lift lid or stir while cooking. Spoon biriani on to a warm serving dish. Garnish with almonds and sultanas and serve immediately. Serve with Onion Sambal (see page 25), Cucumber Salad (see page 24) and hot pickles.

<u>Note:</u> If liked, more colour can be added to dish by garnishing with quartered hard-boiled eggs and cooked green peas.

falooda

There are many versions of Falooda and this is a favourite. It is a sweet drink that may be served with curries. Falooda may also be served as a dessert. A rose-flavoured syrup is mixed with ice-cold milk and poured over jewel-like squares of sparkling red and green agar-agar jelly in tall glasses.

Agar-agar may be bought in powder form by the ounce from chemists and in packets from Chinese grocery stores. It is popular in the East for making jellies and sweetmeats as it sets without refrigeration.

Ingredients	Metric	Imperial
Sugar	400 ml	2 cups
Water	400 ml	2 cups
Rose essence	20 drops	20 drops
Red food colouring	1 teaspoon	1 teaspoon
Crushed ice	for serving	for serving
Jelly:		
Water	600 ml	3 cups
Agar-agar powder	4 teaspoons	4 teaspoons
Sugar	6 tablespoons	6 tablespoons
Rose essence	12 drops	12 drops
Red food colouring	1 teaspoon	1 teaspoon
Green food colouring	1 teaspoon	1 teaspoon

Place sugar and water in a saucepan and cook gently until sugar dissolves. Cool, add rose essence and red colouring. It should be a strong colour as it will be mixed with milk to serve and the resulting colour should be pink.

At serving time, in a large jug, mix approximately 2 tablespoons syrup to each glass of ice-cold milk. Place spoonfuls of coloured jelly into each glass, pour milk mixture over and add crushed ice. Serve immediately.

Jelly: Pour water into a saucepan and sprinkle agar-agar powder over. Simmer gently, stirring continuously until agar-agar powder dissolves, 5-10 minutes. Add sugar and stir to dissolve, cool slightly and add rose essence. Divide mixture between two large shallow dishes and colour one red and the other green. Leave to set. When quite cold and firm, cut with a sharp knife first into fine strips, then across into small squares.

Buffet Party for 20-25
Golden Saffron Rice
Beef Curry
Prawn Coconut Curry
Pappadams
Pol Sambola (see page 43) 4 times quantity
Cucumber Salad (see page 24) 4 times quantity
Tropical Fruit Salad

golden saffron rice

For each person, allow ⅓ cup raw rice. Just remember the rule, allow 2 cups of water to the first cup of rice and 1½ cups water to each additional cup of rice.

If you do not have a pan large enough to accommodate the whole quantity, divide recipe in half and cook it in two saucepans.

Ingredients	Metric	Imperial
Long grain rice	1.6 litres	8 cups
Ghee	5 tablespoons	5 tablespoons
Onions, finely sliced	4 medium	4 medium
Ground turmeric	2 teaspoons	2 teaspoons
Powdered saffron	2 good pinches	2 good pinches
or saffron strands	½ teaspoon	½ teaspoon
Chicken stock	1.75 litres	3½ pints
Salt	2 tablespoons	2 tablespoons
Ground cardamom	1 teaspoon	1 teaspoon
Cinnamon sticks	2	2
Cloves	8	8
Peppercorns	1 teaspoon	1 teaspoon
Sultanas	100 ml	½ cup
Almonds, fried until golden brown in oil	200 ml	1 cup
Peas, cooked	400 ml	2 cups

Wash rice in 4 or 5 changes of water and drain thoroughly. Do this approximately 1 hour before starting to cook.

Melt ghee in a large heavy saucepan and gently fry onion until starting to turn golden. Add turmeric, saffron and rice. Stir and toss rice with a metal spoon until well coated with the ghee. Fry until rice is just golden, approximately 5 minutes. Add boiling stock, salt and spices, stir well. Bring back to boiling point, turn heat to very low, cover pan tightly and cook for 20 minutes. Do not lift lid or stir during cooking time. Turn off heat and leave uncovered for 10 minutes to allow steam to escape.

Just before serving, fluff up rice with a long pronged fork. Garnish with sultanas, almonds and peas.

beef curry

Ingredients	Metric	Imperial
Blade steak	2.4 kg	6 lb
Oil	200 ml	1 cup
Curry leaves	1 tablespoon	1 tablespoon
Black mustard seed	1 teaspoon	1 teaspoon
Onions, finely chopped	600 g	1½ lb
Garlic, finely chopped	6 cloves	6 cloves
Finely chopped fresh root ginger	2 tablespoons	2 tablespoons
Curry powder or paste	8 tablespoons	8 tablespoons
Chilli powder (optional)	2 teaspoons	2 teaspoons
Salt	1½ tablespoons	1½ tablespoons
Vinegar	100 ml	½ cup
Tomatoes, peeled and chopped	2 large	2 large
Fresh chillies, seeded	3	3
Garam masala	2 teaspoons	2 teaspoons

Cut steak into cubes. Heat oil in a large heavy saucepan and add curry leaves, mustard seed and onion. Fry gently until onion is soft. Add garlic and ginger and continue to fry, stirring continuously, until onion is golden. Add curry powder and chilli powder and stir for 2 minutes, then add salt and vinegar. Add beef, mix well together until beef is coated with the curry mixture. Add tomato and chillies. Cover pan, turn heat to very low and cook for 1½-2 hours. (The beef will make its own gravy.) Towards end of cooking time, uncover pan and sprinkle curry with garam masala. Cook uncovered so that liquid evaporates and gravy reduces and thickens.

prawn coconut curry

Prawn Curry is such a favourite that I have included it in this menu as well as in the dinner party menu for 8-10. Make 1½ times the quantity for curry gravy as in Prawn Coconut Curry recipe on page 37 and increase quantity of prawns to 2 kg (5 lb).

Note: It is possible to buy blocks of frozen prawns already shelled and de-veined. If using these, defrost completely and pour off all the water before adding them to the prepared gravy.

tropical fruit salad

Ingredients	Metric	Imperial
Pineapples	3 large	3 large
Bananas	12	12
Lemon juice	100 ml	½ cup
Passionfruit	20	20
Sugar	to taste	to taste
Mango slices	2x565 g cans	2x20 oz cans
Lychees (optional)	2x565 g cans	2x20 oz cans
Fresh mint	6 sprigs	6 sprigs

Cut pineapples in halves lengthways, through fruit and the crown of leaves. With a sharp knife, cut approximately 1 cm (½-inch) in from the skin of fruit and loosen all the flesh. Remove fruit from pineapple shell (it is not necessary to do this in one piece) and discard hard core and any of the 'eyes' that may be left on the fruit. Chop fruit into small dice.
Peel and slice bananas diagonally, sprinkle slices with lemon juice to prevent discolouration. Halve passionfruit and scoop out pulp. Combine pineapple and passionfruit and add sugar to taste. Mix in bananas and lemon juice. Open cans of mango and lychees and drain off syrup. Combine mango slices and lychees with the other fruit. Chill until serving time.

Fill pineapple shells with fruit salad and decorate with sprigs of mint before serving.

Note: In season, use fresh mangoes, peeled and sliced.

menus

These menus are suggested combinations of dishes which will compliment each other. In some of the menus, recipes from one country are combined with recipes from another, and this is quite in order. In South East Asian countries many of the curries and accompaniments are strikingly similar. Serve Vattalappam (see page 48), fruit salad or fresh fruit as dessert. Tropical canned fruits such as mangoes, jack fruit, guavas, lychees, longans and pineapple are particularly suitable.

india

Pilau
Kofta Curry
Tali Machchi
Mixed Vegetable Bhaji
Tomato and Mint Salad
Onion Sambal

Parathas
Lamb Kebabs
Brinjal Bartha
Onion Sambal
Podina or Dhania Chatni
Cucumber Salad

Ras Gulas

Chapatis or Puris
Saffron Chicken
Sukhe Alu
Podina Chatni
Cucumber Salad

Puris or Parathas
Lamb and Potato Curry
or Keema Curry
Cauliflower Bhaji
Brinjal Bartha
Cucumber Raita
Onion Sambal

Vegetarian Meals

Chapatis or Puris
Dhal
Brinjal Bartha
Sukhe Alu
Podina Chatni
Cucumber Raita or Salad

Pakorhas
Kitchri
Cauliflower Bhaji
Cashew Nut Curry
Tomato and Mint Salad
Dhania Chatni

ceylon

White Rice
Pork Badun
Pol Sambola
Chilli Sambol
Prawn Blachan

Kaha Bath or Ghee Rice
Chicken Curry
Fish Curry
Vegetable Curry
Fried Onion Sambol
Brinjal Pahi

White Rice
Crab Curry
Cashew Nut Curry
Prawn Blachan
Cucumber Sambol

Ghee Rice
Pork Badun
Frikkadels
Chilli Sambol
Kalupol Sambola
Fried Eggplant Sambol

indonesia

White Rice
Rendang Daging
Sothi
Onion Sambal
Tomato and Mint Salad

White Rice
Beef Strips, Balinese Style
Opor Ajam
Curried Cucumbers
Fried Sprats

malaysia and singapore

White Rice
Vindaloo
Kalupol Sambola
Fish in Coconut Milk
Fried Vegetables

Nasi Goreng
Country Captain
Eastern Style Croquettes
Cucumber Sambol
Fried Onion Sambol

Mah Mi
Spicy Spareribs
Boiled Noodles or Rice
Braized Mushrooms

White Rice
Malay Satay with Peanut Sauce
Sothi
Sambal Badjak

china

Cold Hors d' Oeuvre
Prawn Ball Soup
Special Fried Rice
Barbecued Loin of Pork

Crab and Egg Soup
Nasi
Chicken with Walnuts and
Snow Peas
Fireworks Prawns
Braized Mushrooms

Agar-Agar Jelly

accompaniments

Besides the fresh chutneys, sambals and salads for which recipes are given, here are some more accompaniments to serve with rice and curry:

Bombay Duck: Not a bird, as the name would suggest, but a fish. It is sold dried in packets and should be cut into pieces and deep fried for a minute or so in hot oil until light golden brown. Crisp and salty, eat it in little bites with mouthfuls of rice.

Dried Sprats: Tiny dried fish sold in packets, the flavour is salty and the texture crisp when fried in oil like Bombay Duck. Sometimes labelled 'Silver Fish' or 'Ikan Belis'.

Fresh Fruits: Ripe bananas are served, sliced and sprinkled with lemon juice, as a foil to a very hot curry. They may be served raw or cut into chunks and fried, and take the place of a sweet chutney.

Unripe mangoes, stoned, peeled and sliced, sprinkled with salt and chilli powder, are also served as an accompaniment, like a fresh chutney. (Or substitute tart apples.) Ripe mangoes are never served with a curry meal, but may follow as dessert.

Pineapple is another favourite fruit accompaniment. Remove 'eyes' and cut into cubes, then sprinkle with salt and chilli powder. Serve chilled.

Fried Nuts: Cashew nuts or almonds fried lightly in oil, drained and sprinkled with salt are sometimes served before or with a meal.

Grated Coconut: Moist, freshly grated coconut makes a delightful accompaniment to curry and rice.

Pappadams: Spicy lentil wafers sold dried in packets. Deep fry one pappadam at a time for 3 or 4 seconds in hot oil. They will swell and turn pale golden. Drain well on absorbent paper. Best fried just before serving, but they may be cooled and stored in an air-tight container if prepared a few hours beforehand.

Pickles, Chutneys and Sambals: There are a number of very good pickles, chutneys and sambals sold in jars. The oil based pickles are most suitable for serving with curry meals.

Prawn Crisps: Also called 'krupuk'. Like pappadams, they need quick deep frying in oil. Made from rice flour and shrimps.

glossary

Abalone: A meaty shell fish about the size and shape of a thick fillet steak. May be purchased fresh or canned.

Agar-agar: A setting agent obtained from seaweed. Available in powder form from chemists or Chinese grocery stores.

Aromatic Ginger: A rhizome resembling ginger, it is sliced and dried, may be purchased in packets. The hard round slices must be pounded with a mortar and pestle or pulverized in a blender before use. It is used only in certain dishes and gives a pronounced aromatic flavour. Must not be substituted for ginger.

Bamboo Shoots: Available fresh in Eastern countries, they are sold in cans in Australia. Large shoots, water-packed, are available halved or sliced. Tiny, finger-size shoots are braized in a delicately flavoured gravy. For the recipes in this book, I have used the water-packed variety.

Barbecued Pork: Sold by the pound in Chinese food stores. Or make it yourself using fresh pork fillets and the marinade for Barbecued Loin of Pork (see page 95). Roast in a moderate oven 170-190°C (350-375°F) about 1 hour.

Bean Sprouts: Mung beans are used for bean sprouts and they are sold in most Chinese stores, either fresh or canned. The fresh sprouts are preferable.

Besan (Lentil Flour): Available in packets from Indian and Chinese shops. Pea flour, sold at most health food stores, may be used in its place, but if pea flour is coarse, sieve before using. Besan has a distinctive taste and ordinary wheat flour cannot be substituted.

Blachan: A paste made from prawns which is used in most South East Asian recipes. Sold in cans or flat slabs. Will keep indefinitely. Also known as ngapi (Burma), trasi (Indonesia) and kapi (Thailand). Available commercially under its Malaysian name, blachan.

Black Cummin: (Bot. Nigella Sativa). Commonly known as kala jeera or kalonji in Indian cookery. One of the five aromatic seeds used to make panch phora. No substitute.

Black Mustard Seed: (Bot. Brassica Nigra.) This variety of mustard seed is smaller than the yellow variety and more pungent. Substitute brown mustard seed (juncia).

Cardamom: (Bot. Elettaria Cardamomum.) Next to saffron, the world's most precious spice, cardamoms grow mainly in India and Ceylon and are the seed pods of a member of the ginger family. If ground cardamom is called for, it is best to have it freshly ground. Used in both savoury and sweet dishes. No substitute.

Cellophane Noodles: Fine, transparent noodles made from the starch of green mung beans.

Chick Peas, Roasted: In the East this is a popular snack. In Australia, obtainable from Greek delicatessens. Used in Burmese food as an accompaniment, mostly in powdered form.

Chilli Powder: The hotter varieties of chilli are dried in the sun, then powdered to make this condiment. Use with discretion.

Chinese Sausages: Dried sausages spiced and filled only with lean and fat pork. Will keep without refrigeration. Steam for 10 minutes or so before serving.

Cinnamon: (Bot. Cinnamomum Zeylanicum.) True cinnamon is native to Ceylon. Buy cinnamon sticks or quills rather than the ground spice which loses its flavour when stored too long. It is used in both sweet and savoury dishes.

Coconut Milk: Liquid extracted from the grated flesh of fresh coconuts, or from desiccated coconut (see page 66).

Coriander: (Bot. Coriandrum Sativum.) All parts of the coriander plant are used in Eastern cookery, but the most commonly used is the dried seed, which is the main ingredient in curry powder. The fresh coriander called for in most recipes is sold as Chinese parsley in some greengrocer shops. If you have difficulty obtaining it, grow fresh coriander yourself in a small patch of garden or even a window box. Scatter the seeds broadcast, sprinkle lightly with soil. Water every day. They take about 18 days to germinate. Pick when about 15 cm (6-inches) high.

Cummin: (Bot. Cuminum Cyminum.) Cummin is, with coriander, the most essential ingredient in prepared curry powders. It is available as seed or ground.

Curry Leaves: (Bot. Murraya Koenigii.) Also known widely as karapincha or

115

karuvepila. As important to curries as bay leaves are to stews. No substitute.

Daun Salam: An aromatic leaf used in Indonesian cookery. Larger than the curry leaf used in India and Ceylon, but has very similar flavour. Substitute curry leaves.

Fennel: (Bot. Foeniculum Vulgare.) Sometimes called sweet cummin, white cummin or large cummin, it is a member of the same botanical family and is used (but in much smaller quantities than cummin) in Ceylonese curries. Available in seed or ground form. Substitute an equal amount of aniseed.

Fenugreek: (Bot. Trigonella Foenum-Graecum.) Available whole or ground. This small, flat, squarish seed, beige in colour, has a bitter flavour and must be used in exactly the stated quantities.

Five Spice Powder: A must in Chinese cooking. This reddish-brown powder is sold in Chinese stores, and is moderately priced. It is a combination of ground anise, fennel, cinnamon, cloves and Szechuan pepper.

Garam Masala: A spice blend added towards the end of cooking for extra fragrance and flavour. Sold in Eastern food stores, but I like to make my own blend. Place each ingredient separately in a dry frying pan and cook for about 2 minutes, stirring constantly; 2 tablespoons whole black peppercorns; 1 tablespoon black caraway seeds; 1 teaspoon whole cloves; 2 teaspoons cardamom seeds; 2 teaspoons fennel seeds. As each one is roasted, turn on to a plate to cool. Put all together into container of electric blender, add 2 small cinnamon sticks, broken into pieces. Cover and blend on high speed until finely ground, or pound with a mortar and pestle. Store in a small air-tight glass jar. No substitute.

Ghee: Clarified butter. Available in tins or tubs, ghee is pure butter fat without any of the milk solids. It keeps 2-3 months without refrigeration and imparts a distinctive flavour when used in cooking. To make ghee, heat butter slowly until melted, stir, remove from heat and refrigerate. The milk solids sink to the bottom of the pan and a thick layer of clarified butter sets on top. Leaving the residue at the bottom of the pan, transfer butter fat to another pan. Heat again until it is boiling, cook for 3-4 minutes. Strain through muslin, leaving any sediment at the bottom of the pan. Pour into a clean dry jar and when cool, cover securely to prevent it absorbing odours. May be refrigerated if desired.

Ginger: (Bot. Zingiber Officinale:) A rhizome with a pungent flavour, it is essential in the majority of Eastern dishes and fresh ginger root should be used. To prepare for use, scrape the skin off with a small sharp knife and either grate or chop finely (according to recipe requirements) before measuring.

Jaggery: See Palm Sugar.

Kemiri Nuts: (Also known as candle nuts.) A hard, oily nut used to flavour and thicken Indonesian curries. Substitute Brazil kernels.

Laos: A very delicate spice, sold in powder form, laos is derived from the dried root of the Greater Galingale. It is so delicate in flavour that it may be omitted.

Lemon Grass: (Bot. Cymbopogon Citratus.) This aromatic plant grows in Australia and is available at some nurseries. It is a tall grass with sharp-edged leaves that multiplies into clumps. The whitish, slightly bulbous base is used to impart lemony flavour to curries. Cut just one stem with a sharp knife close to root, use 10-12 cm (4-5 inches) from base, discard leaves. If using dried lemon grass, about 12 strips are equal to 1 fresh stem, or substitute with 1 strip very thinly cut lemon rind.

Maldive Fish: A dried fish from the Maldive Islands, used extensively in Ceylonese cooking. Sold in packets, broken into small chips, but needs to be pulverized further before use.

Mushrooms, Chinese: These dried mushrooms are quite unlike fresh mushrooms or the dried Continental mushrooms. They are rather expensive but give incomparable flavour. Soak before using in recipes. No substitute.

Palm Sugar: Called jaggery in Ceylon, India and Burma, goela djawa in Indonesia, gula malacca in Malaysia, this dark brown sugar is obtained from the sap of coconut and palmyrah palms and is sold in round, flat cakes. No substitute.

Panch Phora: 'Panch' means five in Hindustani, and panch phora is a combination of five different aromatic seeds. These are used whole and when added to the cooking oil, impart a flavour typical of Indian food. Combine 2 tablespoons each of black mustard seed, cummin seed and black cummin seed (kala jeera), 1 tablespoon each of fenugreek seed and fennel seed. Put into a glass jar with a tight fitting lid, shake before use to ensure even distribution. No substitute.

Prawn Paste: See Blachan.

Prawn Powder: Dried prawns or shrimps, finely shredded, are sold in packets. Buy from speciality food shops or Chinese grocers.

Rampé: (Bot. Pandanus Latifolia.) A long, thin, dark-green leaf with aromatic flavour. Available dried in packets. No substitute.

Raw Sugar: Unrefined sugar, coarse in texture and pale brown in colour. Sold at health stores. Use any coarse brown sugar as a substitute.

Rice: There are literally hundreds of varieties, but the recipes in this book contain three varieties. For Indonesian and Chinese cooking—and these influences are predominant in the food of Malaysia, Singapore and Thailand too—use oval grain rice. This is the small-grained variety commonly used for rice puddings. When properly cooked the grains should be well defined and separate, but clinging together rather than fluffy. For Indian, Ceylonese and Burmese food, long grain rice, properly cooked, gives the fluffy result that is desirable.

Rice Vermicelli: Available in packets from Chinese stores, it is made from rice flour and cooks in a minute or two. No substitute.

Rose Water: Persian and Indian cookery feature this ingredient. Buy from chemists.

Roti Flour: Creamy in colour and slightly granular in texture. Ideal for all unleavened breads. Sold at some health food stores and Chinese stores.

Saffron: (Bot. Crocus Sativus.) The world's most expensive spice, saffron is obtained by drying the stamens of the saffron crocus. The little thread-like strands, hardly an inch long, are dark orange in colour and have a strong perfume. It is also available in powdered form. **Do not confuse it with turmeric which is sometimes labelled 'Indian Saffron'.**

Sambal Badjak: Combination of chillies and spices used as an accompaniment to rice and curry meals. Sold at stores specializing in Indonesian products. Chinese groceries and delicatessens.

Sambal Oelek: Combination of chillies and salt. Used in cooking or as an accompaniment.

Shallots: The member of the onion family known as a shallot in Australia is correctly called a spring onion almost everywhere else.

Snow Peas: Small, flat pods, bright green in colour, they have a very short season but are delightful while they last. The whole pod is eaten together with the tender peas. Used in Chinese recipes. Also known by their French name, mange-tout.

Tamarind: The acid fruit of a large tropical tree. The fruit is shaped like a large broad bean and has a brittle brown shell. Inside the shell are shiny dark seeds covered with brown flesh. Tamarind is dried and sold in packets. To use it as acid in a recipe, a piece the size of a walnut should be soaked in 100 ml (½ cup) hot water for 5-10 minutes until it softens, then squeezed until it mixes with the water. Strain out seeds and fibres. The tamarind liquid is used in given quantities.

Turmeric: (Bot. Curcuma Longa.) A rhizome of the ginger family, turmeric with its orange-yellow colour is a mainstay of commercial curry powders. Though often called Indian saffron, it should never be confused with true saffron and the two may not be used interchangeably.

index

A
ACCOMPANIMENTS 114
Acknowledgements 4
Agar-agar jelly 88
Ajam goreng djawa 72

B
Baked fish 69
Balachaung 58
Balinese style, beef strips 74
Bamboo shoot curry, prawn and 55
Barbecued loin of pork 95
Beef
  curry 110
  curry, dry fried 70
  smoore 39
  strips, Balinese style 74
  teriyaki 100
Bhaji, cauliflower 23
Biriani, mogul 14
Biriani, Muslim style chicken 106
Braized mushrooms 98
Bread, deep fried wholemeal 11
Bread, flaky wholemeal 12
Brinjal bartha 21
Brinjal pahi 46
Broccoli, chicken with walnuts and 97
Buffet party for 10-12 106
Buffet party for 20-25 109
BURMA 50

C
Cashew nut curry 41
Cashew nuts and snow peas, chicken with 96
Cauliflower bhaji 23
CEYLON 31
Chah-zan 54
Chapatis 11
Chicken
  biriani, Muslim style 106
  curry 20
  garlic 61
  in coconut milk 73
  Javanese-style fried 72
  livers with vegetables 97
  saffron 20
  spicy fried 105
  with cashew nuts and snow peas 96
  with walnuts and broccoli 97
Chilli Sambol 44
Chilli sauce 86
CHINA AND JAPAN 89
Chutney, fresh coriander 24
Chutney, ground mint 24
Coconut
  curry, prawn 37, 105, 110
  custard, spicy 48
  ground 67
  milk 66

  milk, chicken in 73
  milk, fish in 78
  milk soup 84
  sambol 43
  sambol, roasted 43
Cocktail savouries 102
Cold hors d'oeuvre 90
Cooked vegetable salad 74
Cooking equipment 8
Coriander chutney, fresh 24
Country captain 86
Crab and egg soup 91
Crab curry 37
Crisp fried vermicelli 63
Crisp semolina shortbread 30
Croquettes, Eastern style 80
Cucumber raita 25
Cucumber salad 24
Cucumber sambol 45
Cucumbers, curried 85
Curried cucumbers 85
Curry
  beef 110
  cashew nut 41
  chicken 20
  crab 37
  dry fried beef 70
  dry potato 22
  egg 17
  fish 17, 38
  fish kofta 56
  fried pork 40
  kofta 16
  lamb 19
  lamb and potato 19
  lampries 36
  meatball 16
  omelet 38
  prawn and bamboo shoot 55
  prawn coconut 37, 105, 110
  vegetable 41
Custard, spicy coconut 48

D
Deep fried wholemeal bread 11
Dhal 22
Dhania chatni 24
Dinner party for 8-10 102
Dry fried beef curry 70
Dry potato curry 22
Dutch forcemeat balls 42

E
Eastern style croquettes 80
Egg curry 17
Egg soup, crab and 91
Eggs, tea 90
Eggplant pickle 46
Eggplant purée 21
Eggplant sambol, fried 47
ENTERTAINING 101
Equipment, cooking 8

F
Falooda 108
Fireworks prawns 94

Fish
  baked 69
  curry 17, 38
  in coconut milk 78
  Indian style fried 17
  kofta curry 56
Flaky wholemeal bread 12
Forcemeat balls, Dutch 42
Fresh coriander chutney 24
Fried
  beef curry, dry 70
  chicken, Javanese-style 72
  chicken, spicy 105
  eggplant sambol 47
  fish, Indian style 17
  onion sambol 45
  pork curry 40
  rice 68
  rice, special 93
  vegetables 85
  vegetables, spicy 23
  vermicelli, crisp 63
  vermicelli, mixed 83
Frikkadels 42
Fritters, savoury vegetable 28
Fruit salad, tropical 111

G
Gado-gado 74
Garlic chicken 61
Ghee rice 34
Gin letho 57
GLOSSARY 115
Golden saffron rice 109
Ground coconut 67
Ground mint chutney 24
Guide, metric 7
Guide, oven temperature 8
GUIDE TO WEIGHTS AND MEASURES 6

H
Halva, potato 49
Hin-chyo 53
Hors d'oeuvre, cold 90

I
Ikan bandeng 69
INDIA 10
Indian style fried fish 17
INDONESIA 65
Ingredients, suppliers of 118

J
Japan and China 89
Javanese-style fried chicken 72
Jelly, agar-agar 88

K
Kaha bath 33
Kalupol sambola 43
Kebabs, lamb 18
Kiri bath 32
Kitchri 15
Kofta curry 16
Kofta curry, fish 56
Kowshwé 58
Kung tom yam 62

L
Lamb and potato curry 19
Lamb curry 19
Lamb kebabs 18

119

Lampries 35
Lampries curry 36
Lentil purée 22
Lentils, savoury rice and 15
Livers with vegetables, chicken 97
Loin of pork, barbecued 95
M
Mah mi 82
Malay satay 77
MALAYSIA AND SINGAPORE 76
Measures, guide to weights and 6
Meatball curry 16
MENUS 112
Metric guide 7
Mi krob 63
Milk
  chicken in coconut 73
  coconut 66
  fish in coconut 78
  rice 32
  soup, coconut 84
Mint chutney, ground 24
Mint salad, tomato and 25
Mixed fried vermicelli 83
Mixed vegetable bhaji 23
Mogul biriani 14
Mohinga 52
Molosaung 59
Mulligatawny 102
Mushrooms, braized 98
Muslim style chicken biriani 106
N
Nam prik 64
Nan khatai 30
Nasi 67
Nasi goreng 68
Noodles, soup 82
Nut curry, cashew 41
Nuts and snow peas, chicken with cashew 96
O
Omelet curry 38
Onion sambal 25
Onion sambol, fried 45
Opor ajam 73
Oven temperature guide 8
P
Pakorhas 28
Panthé kowshwé 51
Parathas 12
Party for 8-10, dinner 102
Party for 10-12, buffet 106
Party for 20-25, buffet 109
Pastries, small savoury 26
Peanut sauce 75
Peas, chicken with cashew nuts and snow 96
Pickle, eggplant 46
Pilau 13

Pilau, rice vermicelli 104
Podina chatni 24
Pol sambola 43
Pork badun 40
Pork, barbecued loin of 95
Pork curry, fried 40
Potato curry, dry 22
Potato curry, lamb and 19
Potato halva 49
Prawn
  and bamboo shoot curry 55
  ball soup 92
  blachan 47
  coconut curry, 37, 105, 110
  soup 62
Prawns, fireworks 94
PREFACE 9
Purée, eggplant 21
Purée, lentil 22
Puris 11
R
Raita, cucumber 25
Ras gulas 29
Rendang daging 70
Rice
  and lentils, savoury 15
  fried 68
  ghee 34
  golden saffron 109
  milk 32
  savoury 78
  special fried 93
  vermicelli pilau 104
  white 67
  yellow 33
Roasted coconut sambol 43
Rolls, spring 87
Rotis 32
S
Saffron chicken 20
Saffron rice, golden 109
Salad
  cooked vegetable 74
  cucumber 24
  tomato and mint 25
  tropical fruit 111
Sambal, onion 25
Sambol
  chilli 44
  coconut 43
  cucumber 45
  fried eggplant 47
  fried onion 45
  roasted coconut 43
Samoosas 26
Satay, Malay 77
Satay manis 71
Satay, sweet 71
Sauce, chilli 86
Sauce, peanut 75
Sauce, Thai shrimp 61
Savoury
  pastries, small 26
  rice 78
  rice and lentils 15
  vegetable fritters 28
Savouries, cocktail 102
Semolina shortbread, crisp 30
Shabu-shabu 99

Shortbread, crisp semolina 30
Shrimp sauce, Thai 61
Singapore and Malaysia 76
Singaras 27
Small savoury pastries 26
Snow peas, chicken with cashew nuts and 96
Sothi 84
Soup
  coconut milk 84
  crab and egg 91
  noodles 82
  prawn 62
  prawn ball 92
  vegetable 53
Spareribs, spiced 81
Special fried rice 93
Spiced spareribs 81
Spicy
  coconut custard 48
  fried chicken 105
  fried vegetables 23
Spring rolls 87
Sukhe alu 22
Suppliers of ingredients 118
Sweet satay 71

T
Tali machchi 17
Tea eggs 90
Temperature guide, oven 8
Teriyaki, beef 100
Thai shrimp sauce 61
THAILAND 60
Tomato and mint salad 25
Tropical fruit salad 111

V
Vattalappam 48
Vegetable
  bhaji, mixed 23
  curry 41
  fritters, savoury 28
  salad, cooked 74
  soup 53
Vegetables, chicken livers with 97
Vegetables, fried 85
Vegetables, spicy fried 23
Vermicelli, crisp fried 63
Vermicelli, mixed fried 83
Vermicelli pilau, rice 104
Vindaloo 79

W
Walnuts and broccoli, chicken with 97
Weights and measures, guide to 6
White rice 67
Wholemeal bread, deep fried 11
Wholemeal bread, flaky 12
Y
Yellow rice 33

120